THE BLESSING CORD

by
Adam Sartwell

**COPPER
CAULDRON**
PUBLISHING

Credits

Writing: Adam Sartwell
Editing: Tina Whittle
Layout & Design: Steve Kenson

For more information visit:
www.coppercauldronpublishing.com

ISBN 978-1-940755-08-3, Second Corrected Printing

Printed in the U.S.A.

TABLE OF CONTENTS

Creating the Blessing Cord.......1

Inspiration.......7

Word.......10

Silent Listening.......15

Praise.......18

Vibration.......22

Insight.......25

Appreciation.......29

Intellect.......33

Awareness.......38

Breath.......42

Desire.......46

Will.......50

Passion.......54

Authority.......58

Change.......63

Vision.......67

Creativity.......71

Daring.......76

Clarity.......80

Incarnate Spirit.......83

Intuition.......87

Flow.......91

Surrender.......96

Compassion.......100

Release.......104

Forgiveness.......107

Love.......110

Expression..114

Dream 118

Blood 122

Stillness 126

Concentration..131

Patience..135

Gratitude..139

Industry..144

Generosity 148

Connection 153

Planning...157

Formation 162

Body..166

About the Author...171

THANKS

No book is completely done just by its author. I have so much gratitude to the people who have supported me through the journey of creating this book. I have to thank my editor Steve Kenson, who held my hand throughout the process of creating this book. He is a great editor and an amazing partner.

I also have to thank Christopher Penczak for inspiring me and encouraging me through the process of creating this book. He is a great inspiration and amazing partner.

I thank the many people who enjoyed the first drafts of this book through my blog and cheered me on. Particular thanks to my biggest fan of this series: Karen Ainsworth. Sometimes I would imagine writing just to her to move through writer's block. Her enthusiasm for creating her own blessing cord and for the meditations spurred me on. Thank you so much for your support, Karen.

Lastly thanks to all my readers. Without you I wouldn't do this. Blessings!

CREATING THE BLESSING CORD

No idea comes out of the void. The inspiration for the blog series that eventually became this book came from the Atlantean rosary work of Dolores Ashcroft-Nowicki that my love Christopher Penczak was working with this year. I watched him get so much from the rosary, but I don't resonate well with the ideas of Atlantis. I wanted to create my own contemplation cord that could be used by Witches and ceremonial magicians.

I was inspired by the Witch's cord which classically was forty knots. I had a great conversation with Christopher where he shared an idea for a contemplation cord using the forty beads and dividing them into the four elements and ten sephira of the Qabalah. Around the time we had this conversation, I was listening to the Elemental Blessing novels by Sharon Shin, which include blessing coins that people used to guide their lives. I took all this information and integrated it into my blessing cord. Focusing on the elemental blessing of the sphere, I created one- or two-word blessings that would guide the expression of the meditation on each cord.

To join in this practice, you will need to create a blessing cord and set aside time to devote to doing the meditations. I have also included in the chapters some contemplation questions for you to think about during the week of each bead.

To make the blessing cord, you need beads of multiple colors to resonate with the ten sephira. I chose to do slight variations with the beads for each element, but that is optional. You could also do some research and use crystal beads that resonate with the sephira of the Tree of Life. I used glass beads because they came in a variety of colors and shapes so I could delineate the element and the sphere. I also added one more bead to the forty to be the bead where the cord joins, making it function like a *mala*. In mantra yoga, the last bead in the mala is called the *merku*. It is not chanted upon or crossed over in chant work. It is supposed to be where all the energy the mantra raises is stored. I liked the idea of this, and since this cord was to bring about more wisdom from the Qabalah, I put a small ceramic skull bead at the end of mine. You can choose your own representation of wisdom or blessings for this end bead.

You will need four beads of each color and a last bead of your own choosing. The colors are white/clear, gray, black, blue, red, yellow, green, orange, purple, and brown. The forty-first bead can be any one you like that symbolizes this work to you. The beads are strung starting with one of white/clear ones and moving through the colors as they are listed above then starting over after brown. I decided to put knots between each bead to keep them separate, but that isn't necessary. When all the colored beads have been strung, tie the two ends together, then string them through the last bead. Tie again and add a tassel, if you like.

The Blessing Cord

The other requirement for this work is to do the meditations. You need to be able to get yourself into a meditative state and then get yourself out of a meditative state. To do this, I have used the Temple of Witchcraft's method of counting down and counting up. If you have another method you enjoy using, go ahead, but realize you may need to modify it to use with the meditations. This work can attune us to the Qabalistic sphere and the elements, so grounding after the meditation is a must. These energies can unbalance us even though we are focusing on the blessings of each.

The following exercise demonstrates how to count yourself down into meditation, then count back up to waking consciousness, then grounding. These are the end caps of the meditations throughout this book. When the meditation says "count yourself down into a meditative state," use the countdown below (likewise with counting yourself up).

Meditative Countdown

Imagine waves of relaxation flowing from your head down to your toes. Focus your attention on each muscle group as you relax. Let any tension flow down out of your body through your toes and into Mother Earth to be recycled. Relax your mind and imagine all your thoughts are clouds being blown away by a gentle breeze. When you have a clear blue sky in your imagination, relax your heart, letting any emotions or stresses flow away. Let the light within your heart and your spirit protect and guide you.

Now we are going to count down into a meditative state by counting down from 12 to 1 and imagining it on the screen of our mind. Bring up the number 12 on the screen of your mind. You can draw it or just imagine it appearing like a movie screen. Now it fades, and you write 11 on the screen of your mind. Draw 10 on the screen of your mind. Getting more relaxed with each number. Draw 9 on the screen. Draw 8 on your screen. Draw 7 on your screen. Draw 6 on your screen. Feeling a deepening relaxation. Draw 5 on your screen. Draw 4. Draw 3. Draw 2 on the screen. Draw 1. You are now in a meditative state where all you do is for the highest good.

Release your screen and count down from 13 to 1, just listening to the numbers and going deeper: 13, 12 ,11, 10, 9, 8, 7, 6, 5, 4, 3, 2, 1. You are now in a journey state and ready to safely explore.

Continue with the meditation of the bead. When finished, use the count-up to waking consciousness.

Count-up to Waking Consciousness

Begin to count yourself up to a waking consciousness by counting first 1 to 13: 1, 2, 3, 4, 5, 6, 7, 8, 9, 10, 11, 12, 13. Begin to wiggle your toes and hands as you begin to come back. Count yourself up again from 1 to 12, coming more fully back into your body with each number: 1, 2, 3, 4, 5, 6, 7, 8, 9, 10, 11, 12. You are now fully awake and refreshed.

Sweep your hands down from your head towards your knees, intending to give yourself clearance of any energy that is not for your highest good. Say either out loud or in your head: "I give myself clearance and balance. I cleanse away all that does not serve. I am in complete alignment with all of my parts."

Grounding Exercise

Visualize a cord of energy, about a foot thick, leaving the base of your spine and dropping deep into the core of the earth. Feel the pressure of gravity all around you. This gravity is now pulling only on that which does not serve your highest good. All unbalanced and unharmonious energy is pulled by this gravity down your grounding cord and into Mother Earth for recycling. Nature abhors a vacuum, so new fresh balanced energy flows up the cord into your body.

Notes on the Meditations

In the meditations you are asked to stretch the screen of your mind around you like a sphere. This is to create a vehicle for you to move quickly through the sephira of the Qabalah. This making of a vehicle harkens back to the Hebrew mystics who used the *merkaba* meditations to move through these energies. The word "merkaba" is sometimes translated as "chariot" or "vehicle." Our modern merkaba meditation is used to make a stronger energy vehicle for psychic exploration.

Each of these meditations uses the Hebrew god name for the Qabalistic sphere of the bead. This is intoned to put yourself in resonance with that particular sphere. Intoning is saying the word with deep concentration and letting it resonate through the body. Each of the god names is written phonetically to help you say them. Remember that these are modern interpretations of how we think ancient Hebrew sounded, so don't get too hung up on saying it perfectly. If you have any qualms about using the Hebrew language, you could use a god or goddess name that you feel resonates with the energy of the sephira.

For your first use of this cord, follow the order of the book. After you have experienced the complete cycle of the meditations and you want to do it again, you can change the order or use divination to determine which one to do next. Here are some suggestions for further use. You could do the meditations from back to front, reversing the flow from manifestation back up to more energetic consciousness. Another option is to focus on a single sphere, doing each of the elemental meditations before moving on to the next sphere. You could even use dice to divine which one you needed on a certain day. You would need a four-sided die and a ten-sided die. Role the dice and use the four-sided die as your "tens" place and the ten-sided die as your "ones" place for a number between 1 and 40, then find the bead that is named and do its meditation. You could also get a small bowl and write out all the names of the meditations on small slips of paper and put them in the bowl. Every day you draw a new blessing from the bowl.

INSPIRATION

The first air bead on the blessing cord is the blessing of inspiration. It is the blessing of Air in Kether. Inspiration means "to take in a holy breath." It is the blessing of an "aha" moment, that instant when we connect fully to spirit and an idea comes to light.

When we think mythically about inspiration, we think about beings who bring us inspiration. Muses, the gods, and angels are all said to deliver ideas that spark creativity. This divine inspiration guides us to our true purpose here on Earth. When you have an idea "pop" into your head, do you ever ask yourself where it came from? Did it come from you, or did it come from a divine messenger?

Inspiration on the cord is the blessing of Air in Kether. Kether is the place on the Tree said to be the closest to the God force. It is a place where there is no shape or form. It is beyond space and time, and yet it is all spaces and times. When we think about the power of air in this space, it is the divine thought. It is the inspiration that comes to us in a place where we think as one with the divine.

The meditation with this bead on the cord is to connect with a person who inspires you, and for a moment, be able to walk in their shoes and perceive the part of their pattern that inspires you. In this exercise, you may either choose someone who inspires you or just be open to seeing who appears when you seek a person for inspiration. Even when you choose a person, it may not be the person who shows up, so be forewarned! In this exercise we use some Qabalistic keys to help us resonate with this gift.

Meditation of Inspiration

Hold the bead of the Kether of Air, the bead of the blessing of inspiration.

Count yourself down into a meditative state.

Resonate the god name of Kether: *Eh-heh-e-yeh.*

Visualize the screen of your mind expanding to surround you in a sphere. You will perceive a rising sensation as the sphere becomes illuminated with a brilliant white light that seems to be filled with all colors.

When the light has filled the sphere, you become aware of a person coming closer out of the light. This is the inspirer whose pattern you need to observe to integrate it into yourself. Greet them. Tell them what you find inspiring about them (if you know what that is). Ask to be able to experience the blessings of their pattern.

If they say yes, look at your spirit body in this light. See how it is beginning to become like this radiant light that has no limits. Allow your light body to flow into this person. You find yourself looking out through their eyes. You're able to share their way of seeing and thinking. You may see scenes of them doing the thing that inspires you. Observe what it feels like to have the experience to do things successfully. Ask your subconscious to remember this pattern, so you can later customize it to your life.

Once again become the limitless light of your soul and flow back out of your inspirer. Relax and let the light re-form into a more inspired you. Give thanks to your inspirer

The Blessing Cord

and ask them if they have any final words of wisdom or inspiration for you. Say your farewells. They fade back into the light of the screen of your mind.

You feel a gentle descent, and the white prismatic light begins to fade from your sphere. Your sphere returns to the screen of your mind's natural size and shape.

Count yourself up into a waking state, making sure to give yourself clearance and grounding as needed. Write down your experience in your journal. Write down all that you remember, without editing or worrying about structuring it too much. Visions, like dreams, can evaporate like dew on a sunny morning. You will want to have as much information as you can.

Take action on the inspiration you received to ground the pattern into your make up.

Contemplation

Where does my inspiration come from? Where do I feel it most? What am I inspired to do in this moment?

WORD

The second bead on the cord is the blessing of the word. It is the blessing of Air in Chokhmah. Many stories of creation begin with a deity speaking to create the world. *Om* is said to be Brahma's first utterance, the sound that created the world. The first chapters of the Bible begin with God's command for things to be. Chokhmah is the sphere of the force. It is my belief that it is the force of this first word that brings energy to creation. We are all part of the Great Spirit, and as such, we have the ability to use the power of the word to bring manifestation of our desires.

In Sanskrit mantra yoga, there are seed sounds that are used to align with a particular energy usually embodied by one of their deities. These seed sounds are called *Bija*. They are primal sounds that can influence consciousness. Om (or *aum*) is just one of these seed sounds. They are usually added to mantras to enhance them.

Om (aum) begins most mantras. It represents consciousness and has the effect of clearing the mind and raising consciousness higher, bringing a deeper *Prana* to the chant.

Eim (I'm) is associated with Saraswati, who rules artistic and scientific endeavors, music and education, spiritual knowledge, memory, and intelligence.

Hrim (hreem) is associated with the feminine force and is used to see through the illusion of everyday reality. It can be used to gain clarity about the universe. It is associated with the heart chakra. It is captivating, bringing both great force and empowerment.

Srim (shreem) is the seed mantra of Lakshmi. It is used to magnetically attract all that is good, helpful, and promoting of positive growth and development. It brings abundance, health, inner peace, financial wealth, friendship, and a love of children and family. It can make your own power to bring these things stronger.

Klim (kleem) is associated with the attraction of a desire. It is often combined with other seed sounds in a mantra to focus the attraction on your goal. This seed sound can be used to manifest what you visualize and focus.

Dum (doom) seed sound is used for the energy of protection. It will help invoke protection and eliminate fear. If repetition of this mantra brings discomfort, stop and try again later.

Krim (kreem) is the seed sound associated with Kali, goddess of creation and destruction. It is used in destruction and liberation mantras.

Gum (gum) is the masculine seed mantra for Ganesha. Use it to remove obstacles and bring success in all endeavors.

Glaum (Glau..owm) is also a Ganesha seed, one that removes obstacles and enhances the energy of will.

Hum ("how" with an "m" on the end) is associated with Shiva. Use it to bring about transcendental consciousness.

Hum (hoom) is another Shiva sound, but is also associated with Agni, the god of fire, and the feminine power of Shakti. It can be used in protection, but it also raises your Prana.

Kshraum (an aspirated but unvocalized "k" followed by a vocalized "sh rau" as in "how" with an "m" at the end) is a seed sound for Narasimha, a manifestation of Vishnu. It is invoked to be rid of stubborn evil situations. It releases your pent-up energies, opens hidden powers within, and is used to destroy indestructible demonic powers.

Ram (rahm) is associated with Rama and brings healing.

Mantra yoga is not the only place we find these words of power. Many different traditions have words they use for different spiritual purposes, including occult and ceremonial orders that have used words of power to create resonance with the aeon they wish to manifest into creation.

Thelema—which means Will—is the word of the law of the Aeon.

IAO is the word of the aeon of Osiris, with each letter standing for a god force: Isis the goddess of creation, Apophis the destroyer, and Osiris the slain and reborn god respectively.

Abrahadabra is the formula for the aeon of Horus for the Great Work complete

Awen (ah-ooh-en) is a Celtic word for the drops of inspiration and wisdom from the cauldron of Ceriddwen.

I AM resonates with the Great Spirit that flows through all things.

You can use any of these in your meditation on the contemplation of the power of the sacred word. You can also use any god's name, any word that is sacred to you, or just a pure vowel sound as long as you choose one with either intention or guidance. A great one to start with is Om or Aum. Almost all Sanskrit mantras start with this sound because it raises our consciousness.

Meditation of Word

Hold the second bead on your blessing cord, the bead of the Air of Chokmah, the blessing of the word.

Count yourself down into a meditative state.

Allow the screen of your mind to expand to surround you in a sphere. Feel a rising sensation as you see gray light or mist begin to fill your sphere. Resonate the god name of the sphere of Chokmah: *Yod heh vauv Heh.*

Float in the gray space and listen. Do you hear any sacred words in the distance? Take this as guidance of the word you are to vibrate first. If you don't hear one, vibrate one of your intentionally chosen words.

To vibrate the word, it is sometimes helpful to elongate the syllables by saying them slowly. You should be saying this word physically as well as spiritually. Let the word flow through your body. Notice how the word feels to you. After a few repetitions you should feel the word as if your whole body was saying it.

Notice how the word makes you feel. Observe any sensations that you receive as feedback from the psychic space around you. Do you hear others joining in with your resonation? What does this word make you perceive?

When you feel you are done, you may feel called to try another word or be satisfied with your work and end the meditation.

Feel a gentle descent as the gray light or mist begins to fade from your sphere. Your sphere returns to the screen of your mind's eye natural size and shape. Count up to waking consciousness

Give yourself clearance and balance. Ground yourself as needed. Write down your experience in your journal.

Contemplation

Every word has an emanation that joins the song of creation; how well have your words served you in creation of your purpose? How would you change them? What is the word that embodies your manifestation in this world?

SILENT LISTENING

The third bead on the blessing cord is the bead of silent listening. It is the blessing of Air in Binah. This sphere is the archetype of the mother, but also of the listener. On the last bead, the god who is the singer calls out a word of creation, giving energy and force to everything. In this bead and sphere, it is given space and form by being heard and understood.

In the teachings of the pyramid of the Sphinx, we are called upon to do four things to become a magus or master: to will, to dare, to know, and to keep silent. Here we focus on silence and the power of listening. In this meditation we ask no questions and seek no answers. We remain silent and just listen to what we "hear" and try to understand. We release our need to do and are allowed to just be.

Within us we have many different aspects of self. Psychology has identified some of these parts. Silent listening is the gift that allows us to open up and hear all the "parts" of ourselves. When we listen to our parts, we can gain understanding of why we may be fighting with ourselves and not getting anywhere with our goals. We can find out why we crave a chocolate after work and even get to the root of the issue, just by listening deeply.

One practice that has helped me in learning more about deep listening is setting aside a time to be silent. This is more than just not speaking or communicating with others in that we also try to limit the information we hear and receive. This time of silence gives us a chance to hear the inner voices of all our parts, allowing us to discern the part that is speaking and who they might be quoting. When we have accepted and then released all they have to say to us, we make space so we can hear the deeper voices of the universe.

Meditation of Silent Listening

Hold the third bead of the cord, the bead of the Air of Binah, the bead of silent listening.

Count yourself down into a meditative state.

Allow the screen of your mind to expand to create a sphere around you. Feel a rising sensation as the sphere begins to lose all illumination until you are surrounded with a black endless void. Resonate the god name of Binah: *Yod Heh Vauv Heh El-oh-heem.*

Let the vibrations of the god name fade into the void. Feel how weightless you are here, as if you were a baby floating in the womb of the great mother.

Begin listening to the black void. At first all you may hear is silence. Just listen. In this space you may hear your own thoughts, the stories of others, guidance, music, or nothing at all. Just listen, and relax. Let any understanding of what you hear unfold naturally on its own. Know that it is okay if it doesn't unfold at all. Relax and listen. Accept all that is offered at this time.

When you feel the experience of this meditation has come to an end, feel a gentle descent as the black color fades on your screen until your screen normalizes in color.

Your screen returns to its normal shape and size. Count yourself back up to waking consciousness.

Give yourself clearance and balance. Ground as needed. Write down your experience.

Contemplation

Are you allowing yourself to just be? Are you listening to others in your life, or are you thinking of what to say next when it is your turn to speak? What are your "parts" trying to say to you? Do you listen to what they are trying to communicate?

PRAISE

The fourth bead is the blessing of praise. It is the blessing of the Air of Chesed, the sphere of mercy, generosity, and expansion. In the element of air, it is expressed when we give and receive praise. Chesed is the home of the archetype of the Heavenly Father, and it is no surprise to me that I would associate the word "praise" with Christianity. Praise has been around longer than the birth of Christianity, however, and has been used not only in polytheism, but in all religions.

Praise is used to give thanks, to commune with deities, to encourage them to intervene in our lives, and to open channels to them. In daily life we give the blessing of praise to each other to do the same. The power of praise can be expanded toward anything in the universe. When we praise, we also empower the thing we are talking about with the power to do just what we praise it for.

Praise also has an effect on us when we use it for others. Our subconscious self is a bit more enlightened than we are and doesn't see a difference between our "selves" and the thing we are praising. So every time we say something about someone or something else, our subconscious thinks we are talking about ourselves. When you praise the things you want in your life, your subconscious hears you and takes action to create that in your life. When you praise the goddess Aphrodite for her beauty and grace, your subconscious begins to think you are talking about yourself.

You begin to see more beauty and grace in yourself. The tricky thing is that we don't always know we are praising something. When you focus on the things you don't want, your subconscious thinks you are praising them. It begins to manifest these accidentally praised things. This is one way that we accidentally create suffering.

When we praise aspects of the gods, we are invoking these aspects in our lives. This means we need to be very careful about what aspects of a deity we call upon. This can also happen with the energies we invoke when we do the blessing cord work. The aspects of the sphere on the Tree of Life we are invoking with our meditation can affect our lives. When I invoke the power of Binah with silent listening, I sometimes feel the ennui that usually accompanies Saturn work for me. Using both clearance and balance and grounding and then moving on to the next sphere helped me mediate these energies.

When we do praise at a meditative level, we empower the praise even more because we are more aligned with the subconscious self. We can mentally program ourselves in this state as if we were in hypnosis. We can use our praise of another to program ourselves for success.

Giving praise is the first part of the meditation that follows. You can also give a blessing with your praise to someone in need. When you work at the subjective level of a meditative state, your praise can become a blessing for another. In my own use of this meditation, I used my praise to bless a friend for the work they did in this world. I praised their sharp mind and clear expression, qualities which they already possessed. I also praised their health and vigor, which at the time was not their experience. This manifested for them in part because of my praise of their health.

The second part of the equation is accepting praise. In our culture we have many unconscious programs about how we accept praise, sometimes preventing it from being truly absorbed. It is important that we actually take in the praise of others as well as give it to others. Remember the lesson of the blessing of silent listening and take in some praise.

Meditation of Praise

Hold the third bead of your blessing cord, the bead of praise, the bead of the blessing of Air in Chesed.

Count yourself down into a meditative state.

Allow the screen of your mind to expand to create a sphere around you. Feel a rising sensation as sky-blue or electric blue light begins to fill the sphere. Resonate the god name of Chesed: *El.*

As the vibrations expand outward from you, call out to a being worthy of praise. You can decide for yourself who that would be or let the Great Spirit guide a being toward you worthy of praise. This person walks toward you through the blue light. You see them surrounded in light. Begin to praise the attributes you most admire about them. Here are some examples you can use, or you can make up your own:

"I praise your keen mind and clear expression."

"I praise you for your open heart that loves me and mine unconditionally."

"I praise your great work in this world that makes others want to shine just as bright."

"I praise your body that is in excellent health and robust vigor. "

These words seem to be filled with the blue light and flow to the being you are praising. You can see them taking them in and feeling your words' blessing. They thank you and begin to recede into the blue light surrounding you.

Say to the blue light all around you, "I am open to the blessing of praise."

In the blue light, you can see images and people who have given you praise in the past. Listen and be open to what they are saying. Really take it in and own that you are worthy of praise. When you feel ready, allow the images to fade.

Feel a gentle descent as the blue light begins to fade from your sphere. Your sphere returns to the screen of your mind's natural size and shape.

Count yourself back up to waking consciousness.

Give yourself clearance and balance. Ground and center as needed. Write down your experience.

Contemplation

How do you react to praise? Where did you learn that response? Is it still working for you? Who in your life do you admire, and are you giving them praise? What about others who are manifesting something you want to create for yourself? Are you praising that accomplishment so you can manifest something like it?

VIBRATION

Everything in the universe vibrates and moves. Even things that seem solid and stationary are moving on the atomic level. The fifth bead is the blessing of Air in Geburah. Geburah is all about power, and the power of air is the power of vibration. It is the power of our vibration that draws or pushes away different experiences and people.

One of the seven Hermetic principles is the principle of vibration, which states that "nothing rests: everything moves; everything vibrates." This constant motion is not just on the physical plane, but on the Spiritual plane as well. Our vibrational frequency draws us to the things that resonate with us. When we meet a new person, we may have a feeling about them before we even talk to them. We might call it a "vibe," either good or bad. This is a reaction between our different vibrational frequencies. Another way you might see it is when you have gone through a personal change and suddenly don't seem to "resonate" with an old friend and, try as you might, you can't seem to keep a friendship that was once easygoing because you don't resonate with each other anymore. Your vibrations have changed.

In this meditation you will explore what it is you have been attracting with your vibration, analyzing if that is what you want, and making a statement to change your vibration to draw to you what you want to create in your life. You may want to design your statement before you go into the meditation. It is basically an affirmation focused on changing your vibration so you vibrate in harmony with something you want to manifest. This is usually a general blessing that aligns with your goals like optimal health, unconditional love, joy, focus, success, or anything you can think of.

Meditation of Vibration

Hold the fifth bead of your blessing cord, the bead of the blessing of vibration, the bead of the blessing of Air in Geburah.

Count yourself down into a meditative state.

Allow the screen of your mind to expand into a sphere around you. Feel a rising sensation as your sphere begins to fill with vibrant red light. Vibrate the god name of Geburah: *El-oh-heem Gi-boor.*

Feel the vibrations intensify around you. Ask to be shown what your current vibration has been drawing and manifesting in your life. Out of the red light, visions or people may appear. Observe how they act. What do they say to you about your vibration as it is right now? Are there changes you want to make? Reach your hand out and feel the vibration of what you have attracted to you. After you feel like you can recognize this vibration, allow the visions and people to fade into the red light around you.

Now you are ready to change your vibration to your goal. Feel your own vibration. Feel it in your body and in your aura. This is your vibration, and you have the power to change it at will. Tell yourself, "I now vibrate in harmony with..." and complete the affirmation with the energy or quality you want. As you say your statement five times, feel your vibration change to be in harmony with your desire. Every cell of your body, every molecule, every particle, now begins to vibrate in harmony with your goal. Your aura begins to change to vibrate with this goal. Let the vibration fill you and pulse out into the universe.

When you are ready, feel a gentle descent as the red light begins to fade from your sphere. Your sphere returns to the screen of your mind's natural size and shape. Count yourself up into waking consciousness

Give yourself clearance and balance. Ground as needed. Write down your experience.

Contemplation

Observe the people in your life and try to feel what they are vibrating in harmony with. How does it manifest in their lives? Observe your own vibration after being with them. How does being around them affect your own vibration?

INSIGHT

The sixth bead is the blessing of insight. It resonates with the Air of Tiphereth, which is said to be the place on the Tree where we have the vision of the Holy Guardian Angel. The Holy Guardian Angel is an intermediary between us and our divine self. The radiant divine self has issues communicating directly to us because it sees time, space, and matter as illusions. Since having an earthly experience requires that we live in time, space, and matter, communing with our divine self is easier through an intermediary shape such as the Holy Guardian Angel. This being is part of us and part of the divine. It descended from spirit so we could be formed, guiding our life toward our great work.

The Holy Guardian Angel can sometimes be confused with the general concept of guardian angels. Guardian angels are often described as beings that watch over us throughout our lives, guiding us when we seem lost, protecting us from harm, and aiding us only if we ask. They are believed to be separate entities, and there is supposed to be one for everyone in the world. They can act as an intermediary between us and other angels. The Holy Guardian Angel is different because it is more like our concept of the Higher Self, the part of us that never left the divine and remains connected to it. They are an integral part of our being that can't be separated from us until we die and are dissolved back into spirit to be reborn.

This all seems like semantics to me because I think spirit by nature is paradoxically experiencing all times, places, and beings in a spiraling, eternal now. The guardian angel and Holy Guardian Angel are not completely separate because spirit doesn't see boundaries. I do believe that we can contact both and by inviting their presence and aid, we can do more than we could on our own. They are companions in our magic. They can give us the blessing of insight because they have been with us from the beginning and will lead us back into spirit at the end of our lives.

In our meditation for this bead, I ask you to invite your Holy Guardian Angel to be present with you and give you insight into your life and guidance along your path of the Great Work. Don't get stuck in what you think your Holy Guardian Angel will or should look like; they can appear as anything because they aren't fixed in any one form. It is also possible for your Holy Guardian Angel to send you a guide instead of showing up itself.

Meditation of Insight

Hold the sixth bead on your blessing cord, the blessing of Insight, the bead of Air in Tiphereth.

Count yourself down into a meditative state.

Allow the screen of your mind to expand into a sphere around you. Feel a rising sensation as your sphere begins to fill with radiant golden yellow light. Vibrate the god name of Tiphereth: *Yod-heh-vauv-heh el-oh-ah Vah-dah-ath.*

Feel how the golden light fills you with a feeling of joy and promise. Call out to your Holy Guardian Angel. Ask for insight into your life and ask for guidance. You see a brilliant light coming out of the distance in the golden light. As it moves toward you, it looks as if it is a being walking toward you. As it grows closer the brilliant light tones down until you can see your Holy Guardian Angel or its messenger guide.

Greet them. Ask again for insight into your life and purpose. Listen to them. They may show you visions and memories or give you insight into solving problems. They may call attention to areas you need to focus on.

When they seem to be done, thank them. Ask if they have a name you can use to call upon them. Thank them again. They begin to depart into the golden light. As they leave, they seem to glow brighter until they are too brilliant to look at. Then their light seems to blend into the golden light of Tiphereth.

Know that if your insight didn't come in this meditation, you should be watching your dreams and looking for omens in your life from your Holy Guardian Angel.

When you are ready, feel a gentle descent as the golden yellow light begins to fade from your sphere. Your sphere returns to the screen of your mind's natural size and shape.

Count yourself up into waking consciousness.

Give yourself clearance and balance. Ground and center as needed. Write down your experience.

Contemplation

Think about the insights given to you about your life by your Holy Guardian Angel. Do they resonate with you and how you live your life? Knowing the messages are filtered through your subconscious, did the messages surprise you?

Or were they things you subconsciously want your Holy Guardian Angel to say? What changes can you make to be more in line with your insight?

APPRECIATION

Appreciation is the seventh bead of the blessing cord. It is the Air of Netzach. In this sphere comes the vision of beauty triumphant. Appreciating the beauty within our selves and our surroundings can bring on spiritual insight. People take for granted the beauty and pleasure in their lives. If they are not putting attention on the things that they want to have in their lives in a positive way, they begin to attract only that which they don't want. By turning our attention to appreciating something, we change our vibration. Taking time to smell the roses, enjoy a good cup of tea, or just tell ourselves how much we love ourselves in the mirror is a practice that can change our relationships to the world and our selves.

Practitioners of some Hawaiian traditions use a technique to gain the attention of the higher self and be able to commune with it. To do this, they think of a beautiful scene or observe something beautiful. They believe that when you are appreciating something beautiful, you begin to raise your vibration to align with your higher self. They use this method before they do a working or prayer. It also raises the vibration of their *mana*, or energy.

When we appreciate the beauty or value of something, we begin to come into a better relationship with it. One of the principles of Huna states that if you can love something just the way it is, then you can be happy with it. For me, "love" is too broad a term, so I use "appreciate." If you can appreciate something, you can be happy with it. All things have a level of consciousness; when we are appreciating something, we are sending high vibrational energy to it. Since everything has a level of consciousness, the thing receiving your appreciation responds. It is through this principle that they find the power of blessing.

When you bless something with the energy of your appreciation, you change it to be in right relationship with you. Take rain, for example. Here in the Northeastern U.S. we have a lot of rain. People cuss out the rain when it comes, and the rain starts to move away from right relationship by coming too often or by not coming at all. If you instead bless and appreciate the rain by thinking about its good points, you come into right relationship with it, and it is more accommodating. Next time you are at the supermarket and it suddenly starts to downpour, start appreciating all that the rain is doing for the earth, your town, how it feels and how beautiful it is. Then when you have established the right relationship with it by blessing it, ask it to let up a bit so you can get to your car. You will be amazed by the result. By loving something as it is, you can come into right relationship with it, and it can change more easily for you.

Meditation of Appreciation:

Hold the seventh bead of your blessing cord, the bead of appreciation, the bead of Air in Netzach.

Count yourself down to a meditative state.

Allow the screen of your mind to expand until it is sphere around you. Feel the sensation of rising as a green light begins to fill the sphere around you. Resonate the god name of Netzach: *Yod-heh-vau-Heh Tza-ba-oth.*

Become aware of your perception of how your energy level feels. Feel the energies of the green light around you. Ask to be transported to a place of beauty. The light seems to recede around you, and you find yourself in a place of beauty. Observe what is around you. Appreciate the surroundings and the beauty within them. See not only the superficial physical beauty, but the marvels of the scene and its place in the grand design of spirit. Spend a little longer than you normally would appreciating the beauty. When you are done, the green light returns to fill the space around you. Once again become aware of your energy level. Has it changed?

Call up the mirror of Venus before you. This mirror can be any kind, as long as it is large enough that you can see yourself and the space around you. Look into the mirror and observe yourself. What do you like best about yourself? Concentrate on that and appreciate it. Send your attention to every amazing thing about you that you can think of. This could be as simple as appreciating the way your hands work. When you feel done making lists of what you appreciate about yourself, check in with your energy level. How does it feel now that you have appreciated the beauty within you?

Behind you reflected in the mirror are some of your friends. They come forward, and as they stand next to you, you can feel a connection to their consciousness. In this space it is easy for you to switch points of view to get an outside opinion of what is appreciated about you. Use this connection to switch your point of view to theirs. See what it is they appreciate about you. When you feel like you have gotten what you need, switch your point of view back to yourself. You may have multiple friends appear in the mirror of Venus. Change points of view easily between them until you are done. Once again check in with your energy level? Has it changed?

When you are ready, you feel a gentle descent as the green light begins to fade from your sphere. Your sphere returns to the screen of your mind's natural size and shape.

Count yourself up into waking consciousness.

Give yourself clearance and balance. Ground and center as needed. Write down your experience.

Contemplation:

When you appreciate something just as it is, do you have the same relationship with it as when you didn't? Can you find the beauty in any given situation? Does finding the beauty change your emotions and your outlook?

INTELLECT

Intellect is the eighth bead on the blessing cord. Intellect is the Air of Hod. This sephira has a great deal to do with the mind, communication, and thought. In Hermetic thought, we are all part of the great divine mind. Since the divine mind is in everything, everything therefore has a level of consciousness to it; everything is alive and responsive. We need to see ourselves as separate entities because without the illusion of limits, we can't function as individuals. Nevertheless, we remain connected to the divine mind at all times. The divine mind makes up many different kinds of cells, like our brain cells make up its own divine "brain." Every part of the divine mind has a function and can be talked to and communicated with. One method of this communication is to go into meditation and speak with its intelligence.

When I use the word "intelligence" in this case, it is to say that there is always a spirit that overlooks any type of manifestation. For example, many New Agers like to call the intelligence of a plant species the *deva* of the plant. This spirit looks after and directs the spiritual medicines and energies of a species of plant. You could think of it as the higher self of the plant or its oversoul. Many believe there is an oversoul or group consciousness that looks after spiritual "families": that would be the intelligence of that group.

So when I use the word intelligence of (fill in the blank), I am talking about its overarching spirit. For this blessing cord meditation, I spoke to the intelligence of my garden to talk about what plans I should make for it this summer. I got advice about what plants to add, which ones to move, and what to fertilize so that what I wanted to grow would come back.

You don't have to limit this communication to plants. You could talk to the intelligence of your place of work, a corporation, your town, your coven, or anything that can be grouped or identified as an individual entity. They all have an overarching intelligence.

Another way intelligence can be used is with the planetary energies in the grimoire traditions. These angelic beings are said to direct and mediate the energies of the seven wanderers of the ancient world, the seven planets and luminaries the first astrologers tracked moving through the sky. Each one has an angelic spirit that watches over its energy, just like a deva would for the energies of the plant species. These are the planetary intelligences listed in Agrippa's *Three Books of Occult Philosophy*:

Nakhiel: Planetary intelligence of the Sun. Good for purposes traditionally aligned with the Sun, such as health, wealth, personality, success, alignment with True Will, and friendship. He is associated with helping to gain success and elevation. He can speed up journeys and bring people to you quickly (an attribute I would associate more with Mercury).

Malka: Planetary intelligence of the Moon. Good with the purposes aligned with the Moon such as emotion, the home, psychic awareness, dreams, and clairvoyance. In addition, Malka's own personal talents include helping people be happy and affable, improving bodily health, increasing wealth. and driving away enemies.

Graphiel: Planetary intelligence of Mars. Good for Martian qualities like hunting, military success, surgery, war, physical strength, courage, lust, athletics and competition. Graphiel's own personal influences can help one win conflicts and bring forward anyone who has a conflict with you. He can teach you how to stop the flow of blood in a wound.

Tiriel: Planetary intelligence of Mercury. Mercury influences business, learning, communicating, writing, medicine, teaching, and any exchange of money or information. Tiriel's personal gifts are helping improve learning, obtaining knowledge, and giving eloquent speeches and presentations. He can help you be more sociable and easy to get along with, and can give answers in dreams and help you avoid poverty.

Jophiel: Planetary intelligence of Jupiter. Jupitarian blessings include wealth, prosperity, mercy, generosity, health, luck, money, and expansion. Jophiel's personal abilities can help with gaining favor of those in authority, appeasing enemies, dealing with difficult situations, and revealing lies and illusions.

Hagiel: Planetary intelligence of Venus. Purposes aligned with Venus are beauty, friendship, attraction, art, music, luxury, love, and pleasure. Hagiel is personally good at ending strife and hardship and gaining love, He also aids conception and can help create or dissolve enchantment.

Agiel: Planetary intelligence of Saturn. Saturn influences the elderly, aging, bones, structures, destruction, death, inheritance, taxes, discipline, and limitation. Agiel can help with safe births and prevent miscarriage; he also can help with influential people like bosses, judges, or anyone in authority.

You can connect to the intelligence of any group of beings with this meditation or connect to the intelligence of a planetary force. It is up to you.

Meditation of Intelligence

Hold the eighth bead of the blessing cord, the bead of intelligence, the blessing of Air in Hod.

Count yourself down into a meditative state.

Allow the screen of your mind to expand until it is a sphere around you. Feel a sensation of rising as your sphere begins to fill with a orange light. Resonate the god name of Hod: *El-oh-heem Tza-ba-oth.*

Feel the mercurial orange light around you like mist. Think of the intelligence you would like to speak with. If you know its name, resonate it; if you don't, just keep thinking about its title. The mist will begin to clear and you find you are in the home of the intelligence you want to speak with. What do your surroundings look like? Do any details stand out to you?

You will see the intelligence you called upon by thought and name. They may come from the misty orange light or may be there waiting for you.

Say hello. Ask the questions you want to ask. Be polite as if you were a guest in someone's home. If you don't know its name, ask if there is a name that the intelligence wants to be called. Ask if there is anything you can do to help it. You might ask if there is a particular symbol you can use to call it in the future.

When you feel like you are done communing with this intelligence, thank it for its time with you. Step back and allow the orange misty light to envelop the intelligence and its home, obscuring it from your sight.

Feel a gentle descent as the light begins to fade from your sphere. It returns to normal coloring and then shrinks back to normal size.

Count yourself up to waking consciousness.

Give yourself clearance and balance. Ground and center as needed. Write down your experience.

Contemplation

Everything has a level of consciousness and intelligence within the divine mind. How is your communication with these intelligences setting you up for success or failure? How can you open up to cooperation with the intelligences around you?

AWARENESS

Awareness is the ninth bead on the blessing cord. This is the blessing of Air in Yesod, the sphere of the Moon associated with the astral foundation of the world of form that we live in. It is also the storehouse of every image and thought that has ever been. It can be an overwhelming place on the Tree because not all that is thought or visualized is necessarily true. This is the place within the Tree of Life that most associated with psychic ability. This is why I bring up the blessing of awareness in this bead.

Here in the physical world, we use only a small fraction of the awareness we have. We are constantly bombarded in our physical bodies by all the five senses, and information is always flowing toward us. We learn to tune out that which doesn't need to be in our conscious focus. We learn to focus our awareness to the thing we are thinking about. This ability to tune out distractions helps us focus in the physical world, but it can also serve more than physical awareness.

Our body is just the tip of the iceberg when it comes to awareness because we are more than just our body. We are a soul, a spiritual being that just happens to be incarnated in a body. Our spirit transcends the physical body and is part of and connected to the Great Spirit. The awareness our spirit can give us is the mass of the iceberg under the surface of the water. With the blended awareness of our spirit, we can become aware of anything in the universe, even things on a different frequency from our own. It gives us a different view of what we are because we can blend our awareness with perspectives outside our own.

I first learned how to do this from a great book on the psychic senses called *You Are Psychic: The Free Soul Method* by Pete A. Sanders. The book has an interesting premise: we have areas of our bodies more sensitive to psychic information, and by focusing our awareness and relaxed attention on these psychic areas, we can experience clearer psychic information. Close to the end of the book, the author explains how to use your soul to expand your awareness beyond your physical self.

The area of soul-shifting is at the back of the head where it meets with the neck. This area is associated with the visions of holy people who seem to have illumination or spiritual energy around the head. It is also the place associated with the doorway that allows spirits to overshadow, be channeled through, and possess a person. In my healing work, it is always a strong spot for those who do trance mediumship. It is a place where parasitic spirits sometimes attach. It is a powerful part of the body where spirit can be channeled, but it is also a strong spot for the spirit to expand from. I use a slightly different method in this meditation because I want us to feel what it is like to be in body first, then what it is like to expand beyond.

This meditation method of expansion can be used to get remote viewing information, to astral travel, to commune with the Great Spirit, and to broadcast a thought out into the universe. When you get good at it, you can even have a bi-located awareness of body and spirit.

Meditation of Awareness

Hold the ninth bead of the blessing cord, the bead of awareness, the blessing of Air in Yesod.

Count yourself down into a meditative state.

Allow the screen of your mind to expand until it is a sphere around you. Feel a sensation of rising as your sphere begins to fill with a purple misty light. Resonate the god name of Yesod: *Sha-dai El-chai.*

Now that you have set the space, begin to feel where your awareness is centered in your body. Allow it to contract to this spot. Gently move your awareness down into your pelvic bowl. Feel what it is like to be in this rooted place within your body. Feel your energies. Relax your focus and allow your awareness to start to flow up your spine, up your back into your neck and to the back of the head where it seems to spread out like a spoon or the hood of a cobra behind the head. Relax your focus even more, allowing it to expand. The key is relaxed awareness. From this place of relaxed awareness, feel your body and your aura. Allow your awareness to expand to be within the chair in which you are sitting. What does it feel like to be the chair resting on the floor?

Let your awareness expand to encompass the room. What does it feel like to be your room?

Allow your awareness to expand gently again to the entire house or building. What does it feel like? What images do you see? Are there any parts where you feel tension in the building? Allow your awareness to gently unfold even more, encompassing your neighborhood and town. Gently be aware of any information coming to you.

Relax and expand your awareness to your country and then even more to the world. What do you sense about the world?

Allow yourself to expand out into the solar system. What do you sense?

Expand to the very limits of the stars. Do you feel the peace in the whirling of the galaxies? In oneness with the All?

When you feel ready, begin to contract your awareness: from the stars, to the solar system, to the planet, to the country, to the town, to the neighborhood, to the building, to the room, to the chair, and finally to the body.

Become aware again of your sphere. Feel a gentle descent as the purple light begins to fade.

Count yourself up to waking consciousness.

Make sure to give yourself clearance and balance and definitely ground in this meditation. Write down your experiences.

Contemplation

If you can blend your consciousness with all that surrounds you, where is the limit of what is "you"? Is there even a limit? Why do we limit who we "are"?

BREATH

The tenth bead on the blessing cord is breath. This is the manifestation of Air in Malkuth, the physical world, where the inspiration that started out in Kether comes into manifestation. Our breath is a powerful blessing from the gods. Not only does it allow us to survive, it can be used to regulate our emotions, change our consciousness, and gather energies for change.

There are many different breathing techniques to master, but in this meditation, I have chosen one of my favorites, which is pranic pore breathing. *Prana* is a Sanskrit term from India which means the energy that is in all things. It is associated with the breath and the power of air. *Pranayama* is the practice of different breathing exercises that raise the prana in your system.

The exercise that follows for this bead in the blessing cord can be used in multiple ways. Just on its own with no intention, it can fill you with the vital energy of prana. It can also be focused by intention to gather a frequency of prana that matches your intention. So you can breathe in the prana of love, peace, joy, harmony, or some other ideal. You can also use it to breathe in energies of Qabalah spheres, planets, or elements by using their corresponding colors or visualizations of their energies. When I set an intention for it, I like to say something to evoke that energy around me so that I can breathe it in. An example would be:

"By the infinite divine manifestations of the Two Who Move as One, I surround myself in the energies of (planet, intention, element, etcetera). May they fill this space so I might breathe them in."

You could also tailor this meditation to your intention using incense corresponding to your goal, such as rose for love, jasmine for psychic awareness, frankincense for healing and protection, or red sandalwood for peace. I like to do this exercise outside because I feel the Prana is clearer and more energized by nature. It will work inside too, but it really rocks outside!

Pore breathing concentrates on your skin and pores to breathe in the energy that is all around you. This meditation can be enhanced by wearing light clothing or going skyclad, but works perfectly well clothed. I have done this one in the middle of a snowstorm in January in northern New England with all my winter layers on, and it worked perfectly, so don't get too worried about what clothes to wear (or not wear).

One of the dangers of this exercise is that you can overload your body with prana. Using the grounding and centering techniques at the beginning of this blog will help make sure you don't blow your circuits. If you are working with one of the elements or one of the planetary energies, it is recommended that you don't work with one energy too much because you can unbalance yourself and your relationship to the other planets and elements. This exercise can also be used to gather energy to fulfill a spell or creative visualization. To do this at the end of the meditation, imagine the energy you have gathered being

The Blessing Cord

sent from your hands, third eye, or heart to your visualization of your end goal until it glows with the energy of the prana you sent.

Meditation of Breath

Hold the tenth bead on the blessing cord, the blessing of breath, the bead of Air in Malkuth.

Count yourself down into a meditative state.

Allow the screen of your mind to expand out around you forming a sphere. Feel the slight shift as a garden begins to grow up around you in the sphere of your mind. Resonate the god name of Malkuth: *Ah-do-nai Ha-ah-retz.*

Bring your focus to your skin. Imagine the pores of your skin are becoming more open and porous. You may feel a slight tingle all over your skin as it begins to open a bit more.

You can evoke the energy or intention you are working on now with this short evocation while visualizing the energy filling the room:

"By the infinite divine manifestations of the Two Who Move as One, I surround myself in the energies of (enter your intention here). May they fill this space so I might breathe them in. So mote it be."

Begin to breathe in the energy around you from your newly opened pores. Imagine the energy filling you as you breathe in. Hold your breath for the count of three to let your body absorb it. As you release your breath, you are breathing out the opposite of the energy you just breathed in. As it leaves your body, it is dissolved and flows away from you. Breathe in the energy of your goal, repeating the process until you feel "full" of this energy.

You can send this energy out toward a goal or just absorb it into your body.

When you are done, focus on grounding any excess energy into the earth to be recycled. When you feel more grounded, imagine that your pores are returning to a normal amount of openness.

Become aware of the garden around you in your sphere. Allow it to fade as you feel a slight shift. Your screen of your mind returns to its normal size.

Count yourself up into waking consciousness.

Give yourself clearance and balance and ground some more if necessary. Write down your experience.

Contemplation

In all types of situations, bring attention to your breath. Is it relaxed? Is it hectic? Is it appropriate for the situation you are in? Does changing the breath change your experience of this situation?

DESIRE

Desire is the first bead of the fire quarter of the blessing cord. It is the blessing of the Fire of Kether. While doing my course of study with the Temple of Witchcraft, I had a profound vision when we were meditating on Chokmah of what I call the Holy Desire. It was a version of why everything in the universe was created.

In the beginning there was nothing but Kether, and because the Great Spirit is everywhere without limits, it could experience nothing. So it separated with a spoken word, one part of it speaking and one part listening. This yearning for experience is the Holy Desire. From this one desire, all was created and continues to be created, preserved, and destroyed. This desire also made a multitude of expressions and experiences all had by the Great Spirit in Kether because the separation is always followed by return and reintegration, and the Great Spirit still has no limits, but can experience them through us and everything that is.

I wrote this poem about it:

Holy Desire
From nothing and all
the holy desire
of self on to self
the speaker to the listener
the word divided us
in it we found

joy and sorrow
pleasure and pain
laughter and tears
and through them
our love is made pure
of self on to self
our holy desire
for nothing and all.

Meditation of Desire

Hold the eleventh bead of the blessing cord, the bead of desire, the Fire of Kether.

Count yourself down into a meditative state.

Visualize the screen of your mind expanding into a sphere around you. Resonate the god name of Kether: *Eh-heh-e-yeh.*

You feel a rising sensation. Your sphere begins to fill with radiant opalescent light that seems to hold all colors inside it. As the light begins to wash over you, feel your own limits beginning to dissolve into the oneness of the Great Spirit. Express your desire to experience the Holy Desire that created the universe and the more personal and particular Holy Desire that your life fulfills.

You may feel a shifting expansion as you move through time and then a concentration until everything seems to be in one point, one "place," one "time." Feel the limitless oneness of this time before time. Connect to as much as you can and feel the Holy Desire of the Great Spirit. Know that we as beings of space and time may experience it in the way our subconscious mind can explain it, through our own symbols and experiences.

Now move forward in time to when the Holy Desire builds to a crescendo and the word is uttered and heard. You may experience a rush of expansion and a separation as one part speaks and the other parts of you listen. Continue down the new flow of time, seeing some of the Holy Desires as they create, become destroyed, and reintegrate into the one. This is the alchemy of creation and destruction.

Now focus your mind to the time just before your birth. Feel again the oneness of the Great Spirit and sense the Holy Desire creation wanted to fulfill in you. This may come to you in symbolic form. If you don't perceive anything, know that you may see it in a dream later as the vision filters into your consciousness. Know that this Holy Desire that brought you into being changes all the time and is more complex than our human minds can fully comprehend. We fulfill these Holy Desires just by being our true selves.

Once you feel like you have gotten a sense of the Holy Desire that created you, move forward in time until you are in the here and now. Experience again the radiant opalescent light of Kether filling the space around you. It begins to recede, leaving the sphere of your mind as you feel a gentle descent. Allow your screen to return to its normal size.

Count yourself up to a waking consciousness.

Give yourself clearance and balance. Ground and center as needed. Write down your experience.

Contemplation

What is the Holy Desire you express? Why did spirit choose to form into the being that is you? Can you ever truly fulfill this desire? Does this experience of the Holy Desire change your own concept of self and your purpose?

WILL

The twelfth bead on the blessing cord is the blessing of Will. The blessing of Will is the Fire of Chokmah. In Western mysticism, there is the concept of two different types of will. There is the personal will we use to go through our daily lives and complete our own desires in this world. Then there is the Divine Will which is what we use to go toward our Great Work. The Great Work is the reason we are here in the first place. It stems from that Holy Desire we experienced in the last meditation. Divine Will is usually capitalized to denote that it is the greater or True Will. Our personal will may not always match our Divine Will. This is where we start to get off the track that spirit wants for us.

For example, say the divine wanted to experience a creative artist. The Divine Will of the person created to carry out this desire is designed to be artistic. This person goes through many experiences throughout their life and decides through personal will that they would rather be an investment banker instead of a artist. That person will never feel like they are living up to their full potential. Spirit has ways of telling this person they are in the wrong field, but those signs are not always followed. For this example, the person finds that they have been fired because the company they have given their time to is implementing cutbacks. They apply to different places, but can't seem to get back in the door. While all of this is happening, they see a sign for an art class and remember how good it felt to paint, and they want to feel it again. So while they are searching for a bank, they begin to paint. They paint all their feelings out onto the canvas: all the despair, moments of happiness, and all that they are experiencing. The class has a small art show at the end that is visited by an art dealer who is taken by the art of our divine artist and offers to represent them.

This is a bit of a simplistic example, but it gives you a taste of how Divine Will can make you feel more yourself when your personal will is in alignment with it. The meditation for this blessing is about clearing ourselves of anything that is not in alignment with our Divine Will.

The inspiration for this meditation is from Vivianne Crowley's *The Magical Life,* where her own meditation of Will uses the chakra system, aligning it with the planetary energy of Mars. Since the meditations in this book use the system of Qabalah, I have adjusted my version to go through the Tree one pillar at a time within the body of the practitioner.

Meditation of Will

Hold the twelfth bead on the blessing cord, the bead of Will, the blessing of Fire in Chokmah.

Count yourself down into a meditative state.

Allow the screen of your mind to expand around you to form a sphere. Resonate the god name of Chokmah: *Yod heh vauv Heh.*

You feel a rising sensation as the sphere begins to fill with gray misty light all around you.

Above you, you see a great ball of opalescent white light. It begins to descend until it is directly above you. A beam of light begins to emanate from it, connecting to the space just above your head. As it touches this space, a sphere of light seems to open to it just above your head. You feel a cleansing of this space where Kether resonates in your body. The beam fills up this center until it is completely cleansed of all that does not serve your Divine Will. The beam then begins to flow down into your throat, cleansing the space that is Da'ath, the eleventh sphere. The white light begins to fill this space, clearing it of all that is not in alignment with Divine Will.

The beam descends into the area of your heart, awakening and clearing the space that is Tiphereth of all that doesn't serve. Then it descends into your pelvic bowl. Here it begins to clear Yesod within the body. The beam descends further down into a sphere just beneath and around the feet that connects you to this world, the sphere of Malkuth within the body. This area is cleared of all that does not serve your Divine Will. Let the beam descend further out into the earth below you.

Bring your attention back to the sphere above you as the light begins to flow down the right side of your body. At the right side of your head it touches the sphere of Binah, cleansing away all that doesn't serve. From here it flows down to cleanse Geburah at your right shoulder. The beam descends down to just above your right hip, cleansing Hod. When this area is cleansed, it flows down the right side to your feet, down through Malkuth.

Bring your attention back up to the ball of light as the beam expands and flows down the left side of the body. It flows to the left side of the head, cleansing the area of Chokmah. The cleansing flow descends down into your left shoulder, cleansing the sphere of Chesed. When it is cleared and aligned with Divine Will, it flows down into just above the left hip to cleanse Netzach. The beam cleanses this area and then descends again to Malkuth.

Feel the cleansing beam expand again. Sense the current of Divine Will cleansing you of any thoughts, feelings, or complexes that are blocking your Divine Will. Feel purpose begin to fill your every particle, filling your aura and your entire energy body. The flow expands until you are encased within a column of pure Divine Will and purpose. Ask yourself, "What is my Will?" Let your mind clear and be open to receive answers in the form of sensations or visions. Just experience these freely and allow analysis to come later.

Become conscious again of the gray misty light around you. Feel a gentle descent as it begins to fade, and your sphere becomes its normal color. Allow the screen of your mind to return to its normal size.

Count yourself up into waking consciousness.

Give yourself clearance and balance. Ground and center as needed. Write down your experience.

Contemplation

What is your Will right now? Is your own personal will in alignment with your Will? Why or why not? What action could you take right now to enact your Will?

PASSION

Passion is the blessing of the third of the fire set of beads and the thirteenth in the blessing cord. The blessing of passion is the Fire of Binah. In this blessing the Holy Desire sparks will, and when it goes into the forming power of Binah, it becomes passion. Passion brings creativity and fertility, and it builds in power to overcome resistance. When passion for our Holy Desire becomes powered by our will, it brings us into alignment with our own divine essence.

Passion for art, music, learning, or anything else rewards us with enjoyment and the peace of knowing we are fulfilling something within us. Passion can be creative or receptive. You could be passionate about doing theater or going to see theater productions. Do not limit how your passion can manifest.

Many times we move away from our passions because of the needs of our daily lives. We get wrapped up in making money and seeing to the needs of our partners, parents, and children. We stop focusing on the passions that lead us to our end goals and get mired into our means goals, the things that help us survive, like getting and keeping a job. We soon forget that our means goals are just things that are the means to the end goals of what we truly value and are passionate about doing with our lives.

With every passion there is resistance. There are obstacles and setbacks. Every incubating chick in an egg has to muster enough passion for life to break free of its shell. The shell protects it while it grows, but once it grows enough to be uncomfortable with its limitations, it begins to push against the egg and break free into experiencing its passion. Resistance can be something that holds you in your egg, but it can also be the challenge to embrace your passion and build your strength so that you can escape into greater passion and fulfillment. We need to stop fearing our resistance and see it as a sign that we must build the strength of our passion to break through it.

In this meditation you will connect or reconnect to your passions and be able to recognize the places where you feel resistance to them being fulfilled. In it we will train the mind to build passion until it overcomes resistance.

Meditation of Passion

Hold the thirteenth bead of the cord, the bead of the Fire of Binah, the bead of passion.

Count yourself down into a meditative state.

Allow the screen of your mind to expand to create a sphere around you. Feel a rising sensation as the sphere begins to lose all illumination until you are surrounded with a black endless void. Resonate the god name of Binah: *Yod Heh Vauv Heh El-oh-heem.*

In the inky blackness, you see a shape forming before you. It looks like a inky blue pod growing out of the darkness. The pod resembles a giant rosebud that has not yet opened. This pod holds your passions. Touch the pod and call out to your own passions to manifest within it.

A light grows within the pod, and its sides become clearer and brighter, eventually becoming translucent. Within the pod, you can see yourself engaging in your passions, those things that feed your soul. The images of your passions are filled with color and intensity. Even from the outside of the pod, you can feel the intensity of the passion contained inside. Imagine that the contained passion is growing in strength until the light of the images is so strong you can hardly see it.

Reach forth again and step into the pod and feel the intensity of your passion. Give yourself time to feel it fully. Experience the passions that feed your soul and allow you enjoy your life. Let the passion integrate with your being until you feel that you are being contained and need to break free.

Bring your attention to the sides of the pod around you. Reflected on the sides of the pod are the reasons and excuses why you have not been fulfilling your passions. Observe these reasons as flittering images. Know that these are the resistance that is helping your passion grow in strength and not obstacles in your way. After you feel you have observed them, say to these images, "You are the resistance that builds the strength of my passion. I will blossom into who I am meant to be."

Return your attention to the passion building in you. Feel it like an energy growing in intensity until it suddenly causes the edges of the pod to curl away from you at the apex of the pod. As the energy builds, the pod blooms out into a flower below you, and your passion seems to radiate out of you as if you are a star-bright jewel within this flower. Feel what it is like to be this radiant being of pure passion and delight. Look around; you may see other pods opening and awakening to passion, seemingly in response to your opening. They may look like stars within the inky void.

When you are ready to return, let the images fade, knowing you can call up this passion at anytime. You will know that when you feel resistance, it is just building your passion.

As the lights fade and the void fades, you feel a gentle descent. Your screen returns to its normal shape and size.

Count yourself back up to waking consciousness.

Give yourself clearance and balance. Ground and center as needed. Write down your experience.

Contemplation

In what way does your passion manifest: art, poetry, herbalism, writing, reading, learning? Do you express this passion in your life? What is the resistance that is helping you build your passion so you can overcome it and express it even more strongly?

AUTHORITY

The fourteenth bead in the blessing cord is the blessing of authority. It is the Fire of Chesed. Authority is the power of sovereignty and inner mastery. We have the ability to be sovereign in our lives, or we can give our power away to others and to circumstance. The more authority we exert in our lives, the more we can make changes in our lives and be better examples of how life can be to others.

Oftentimes, we don't want to be the deciding factor in our lives. We let others choose what to have for dinner, where we go on vacation, how our governments are run, and a million other decisions. It feels easier to just release the responsibility for our lives to our partners, our families, our teachers, and to our government. We can then blame them instead of taking responsibility for our choices. Even the surrendering of choice is a choice, however, and we are still responsible for how it turns out when we give our decision-making power to another.

An enlightening viewpoint I learned from the Silva Mind Control method is that we can always talk ourselves into or out of doing anything. We often come up with reasons and excuses for why we are not doing something or why we want to do something. The only reason we truly need is that we want or don't want to do something. We add to our mental to-do list things that we think we "should" or "ought" to do, what we think others want us to do or what would be the "right" thing to do. But as my friend Matooka says, "Don't should on yourself."

We also need to have the authority and mastery of our lives to be able to give ourselves permission to take a break. With my own busy partners, I have had to ask them why they can't give themselves permission to relax. Sometimes I jokingly say, "I give you permission to relax today and just enjoy" as if I were the king in the situation. But it does illustrate how we are each inner sovereigns of ourselves and the ways we manifest that by giving permission.

In this meditation I use some words of power, which is a method of using a declaration or a grouping of affirmations to manifest change. I learned about it from the books of Marion Weinstein. The concept is that you begin by invoking spirit, stating within that the spirit is or contains a manifestation of what you want to become, that you are either in alignment with that greater spirit or an embodiment of that spirit. Then you speak your affirmations of what you want to be. A statement of release and transformation follows for the energies you have released in the past that are not in alignment with your goal, turning them into whatever your goal actually needs. Add caveats for the work to harm none and that it be for the highest good. Lastly, make a declaration of it with a phrase like "so mote it be" or "so be it" or "amen."

These words of power can be used to manifest anything. They are even more powerful when spoken in meditation for they are delivered to the deepest parts of the self faster that way. Within the following meditation, you are given some words of power to speak in a sacred inner temple.

Read them over and make sure you have the gist of them before you do the meditation. Give yourself the authority to change them to suit your aesthetic.

Meditation of Authority

Hold the thirteenth bead of your blessing cord, the bead of authority, the bead of the blessing of Fire in Chesed.

Count yourself down into a meditative state.

Allow the screen of your mind to expand to create a sphere around you. Feel a rising sensation as sky-blue or electric blue light begins to fill the sphere. Resonate the god name of Chesed: *El.*

Around you a temple begins to come into shape. This is the temple of your inner authority. You are sovereign and master within this temple. It may resemble your inner temple or a place in your life where you feel in control and commanding. Look around and observe this place. Are any of your guides or spirits present here to witness? Here is the place to invoke the words of power to proclaim mastery over your life. You can use the words of power that follow or you can make up some of your own:

"I call upon the Goddess, God, and Great Spirit
who contain within them true authority, mastery, and sovereignty
of which I, (name) am an embodiment,
to hear this declaration:
I am the sovereign of my life.
I grow into greater self-mastery every day.
I take responsibility for my choices and make corrections

when needed.

I am the greatest authority when it comes to me.

In humility, I ask to be crowned in wisdom, power, and compassion.

I release and transform all that does not serve to become greater self mastery.

All aspects and parts of me work in harmony toward self-mastery

for the highest good with free will to all, harming none.

So mote it be!"

After your proclaimed words of power, you may hear an astral bell or just the words moving outwards and echoing in the temple as if the whole universe is listening. There may be shifts within the temple or things that are suddenly changed about it. Observe these changes to interpret them —like dream messages or omens about your own path to mastery. Thank any spirits or guides who have joined you in this place.

The blue light begins to fill the temple until the temple fades to blue. Then the blue light begins to fade as you feel a slight descent. The screen of your mind begins to go back to its normal size and color.

Count yourself up into waking consciousness.

Give yourself clearance and balance. Ground and center as needed. Write down your experience.

Contemplation

Where do you need to take more responsibility for your life? What is it you have been putting off? Are you taking care of yourself as well as others? Do you feel like a sovereign in your life?

CHANGE

The fifteenth bead in the blessing cord is the blessing of change. This is the Fire of Geburah. Change is a constant in the universe. Nothing stays the same forever. Some things come back around, but eventually they change again. We can't escape being changed by the circumstances of our lives. We are constantly growing, building, deteriorating, or decaying.

One of the teachings we can draw from the images of Baphomet by Elphias Levi are the words written on Baphomet's arms: SOLVE and COAGULA are the Latin words meaning "to separate" and "to join together" respectively. Since Baphomet is a microcosmic view of the universe, neither male nor female, human or animal, it represents this power of change in the universe in these two concepts. These are the two sides of change: to separate or divide into its component parts or to bring things together in a new shape or configuration. These processes are the two methods the alchemist uses to create a pure essence of the substance they are working with. This is why nature is considered the greatest of alchemists.

Change often has a rhythm and a cycle to it. These cycles of change are the small cycles that reflect the greater cycles of life. Take, for example, the life of a tree. Spring is birth and renewal, summer is the prime of life and growth, fall is the decay and waning, preparing for sleep or death, and winter is dormancy and death—each has its place and is a reflection of the whole life of the tree. None is good or bad; it just is. No part of the cycle could happen without the other parts of the cycle. In this meditation, we go through the life of a tree to feel the rhythms of change and experience how an end is not just an end, but also a new beginning.

Meditation of Change

Hold the fifteenth bead, the bead of the blessing of change, the blessing of Fire in Geburah.

Count yourself down into a meditative state.

Allow the screen of your mind to expand to create a sphere around you. Feel a rising sensation as the sphere fills with a red light. Vibrate the god name of Geburah: *El-oh-heem Gi-boor.*

The red light around you transforms into the red mist of dawn in a grove of oak trees. Look around you at your feet and find an acorn. Take that acorn and dig a hole in the earth for it. Once it has been buried, let your body dissolve and become like liquid light. You pour yourself into the buried acorn. All your essence is within this acorn. Merge with this small life.

At your will, project yourself and your acorn through time so you can move through its life cycle. Feel the resistance as acorn-you grows roots, displacing the soil. Feel the resistance as you grow to break through the soil to the surface. Feel the growth as you become a young sapling. Sprout leaves to soak in the summer sun. As summer wanes, you drop these leaves to prepare for the sleep of winter. What does it feel like to give up this part of yourself, returning it to the earth? Sleep well under the snow, until spring rises again and you bud and begin to grow again to feel the summer sun.

Your branches grow, only to have one branch break and fall off because of the wind. You persevere, knowing that the loss of this branch has opened up that space to let your other branches get even more sun. As fall and winter come again, time marches forward at an even more rapid pace. You feel what it is like to grow up above the other trees. Grow and grow, season by season, until you are a gigantic oak sheltering smaller oaks of your own. What is it like to have come into fertility?

Time marches forward to when your vitality begins to wane. The processes you have gone through become harder and harder until your tree begins to die and decompose. Feel the separation of spirit from the body of the tree, how it spreads and expands, feeding the spirit around it. Know that this is not the end, only a new beginning, for this tree soul.

The liquid light of you begins to separate from the tree spirit and reform into your spirit body. Take time to ground yourself into the shape that is you. Thank the tree spirit for teaching you the ways of change and its cycles.

The red light begins to fill your sphere again, blotting out the grove. You feel a gentle descent as the red light fades. Your sphere returns to the shape and size of the screen of the mind.

Count yourself up into waking consciousness.

Give yourself clearance and balance. Ground and center as needed. Write down your experience.

Contemplation

What changes have you gone through in your life? How has this affected your journey? What changes do you need to make to create a better life for yourself and others?

VISION

The sixteenth bead of the blessing cord is the blessing of vision. This is the blessing of Fire in Tiphereth. A vision gives us guidance along our path. It can give us the ability to choose, to embrace a new way, to let things go that no longer serve, and can give us new awareness. Visions have been sought out since ancient times. People with the "sight," like the oracles of Delphi, were consulted for their gift of vision. Native Americans and other tribal cultures used the vision quest to find spirit guides, both for healing and to gain the knowledge needed to attain adulthood.

Our modern culture seeks its answers in the human experience. We turn to books, to the internet, to our teachers, and all other places in the material world. We have forgotten that there is only so much a book, class, or online collection of information can teach us about ourselves and our perception of the world. We find ourselves searching and searching for something to guide us, in book after book, on site after site, until we give up hope.

What we seek is vision. We seek out sacred knowledge from the All, but we can only find reflected visions of our personal vision in others. We have to go out and experience the vision and be guided by our own knowledge of the truth. As the Charge of the Goddess says, "that if that which thou seekest thou findest not within thee, thou wilt never find it without thee."

There is an element of trust and confidence inherent in this leap to find our own vision. We must trust our own abilities and knowledge. Our confidence must be high enough to know we can seek our own vision and find it. We must trust in the universe, divinity, and the spirit world that we will be able to find our vision. This is what the books of techniques, internet sites, teachers, and all other reflections of the vision prepare us to do—seek out our own vision of what we are and what we are here to do.

This meditation is a vision quest. You can use it to gain guidance on anything, but you must have a clear intention of what you are seeking. The intention can be something as broad as "show me what I most need to know" or as defined as "show me the animal guide that is working with me right now." It can be anything where you seek guidance.

Meditation for Vision

Hold the sixteenth bead, the bead of the blessing of vision, the blessing of Fire in Tiphereth.

Count yourself down into a meditative state.

Allow the screen of your mind to expand into a sphere around you. Feel a rising sensation as your sphere begins to fill with radiant golden yellow light. Vibrate the god name of Tiphereth: *Yod-heh-vauv-heh el-oh-ah Vah-dah-ath*

The golden light begins to lose its opaque nature, and you can see that you are in a field of golden wheat. The sun is bright, and you see a large tree not far from where you stand. Sunlight plays through its branches. This tree is the World Tree, greatest of all guides, for it is a part of all, touching upon all worlds. Walk toward the tree. See the light play through the branches. Feel the bark of the tree. Feel this ancient being's pulse of life. Tell the World Tree your intention to gain vision. Tell it all about what you are looking for. The tree may respond by opening a gateway in its roots or you may become aware of a path; it may even call an animal or spirit to guide you.

Follow the path of your awareness. Be aware of the surroundings as you pass through: are there any plants or animals that stick out to you as you walk the path? These details can be as guiding as they are in dreams, because they may be symbols of your vision.

Follow the path until you come to the place where your vision awaits you. Let the landscape and the beings within it guide you. Anything is possible in the spirit world. If you don't understand a part of the vision, begin to talk to it and ask what it represents. Even the inanimate has consciousness and can respond in the spirit worlds. Observe the details of your vision.

When you have gained all the vision you feel you are going to receive, give thanks to the spirits and the world around you for their guidance. Return by the path you took back to the World Tree. Thank it for its aid. Walk back to where you began the vision quest.

Golden light again begins to fill the area around you, making the world go opaque with the intensity of its light. As the light fades, you feel a gentle descent. The screen of your mind begins to return to its normal size.

Count yourself up into waking consciousness.

Ground and center yourself. Write down your experience.

Contemplation

Where have you gained vision in the past? Use dream interpretation books, free association, and your own knowledge of your symbols to interpret your vision. What do you need to do to enact this vision?

CREATIVITY

The seventeenth bead of the blessing cord is the blessing of creativity. This blessing is the Fire of Netzach. This Venusian sphere is the place where our emotions and feelings are expressed in art, beauty, or creativity. With creativity we give new forms to old energies, new life to our creations, and are able to reflect on our experiences through the medium of our choosing.

With each creation there is a destruction, as that which was unfolds into a new creation all its own. Sometimes we fear destruction of the old, and we hamper our creativity. We can fear what it will be like when we create something new from the old. Fears may arise as to what this creation's impact on the status quo will be. Don't let fear stop you from creating something you are passionate about.

A fact of life is that everything comes to an end. Each act of art or creation is impermanent. It will eventually change or be destroyed. Entropy eventually returns a creation back into the soup of energy so it can be used again to create something new. It is also a fact that every ending is a new beginning. Our newest creation is built out of all of the experiences and energies we have put into making it. When we create anything, we destroy something else. When we destroy, we liberate new energy to create again.

This is not just a spiritual principle, but an energetic one as well. We are constantly creating thought-forms in our energy body. These thought-forms dissolve back into our energy over time if they are not maintained by the energy of our attention. A thought-form is the blueprint for manifestation of that thought into reality. Author and teacher Orion Foxwood has a saying: "What is on the altar of your mind?" Every one of these created thought-forms is a prayer on the altar of your mind. Sometimes these thought-forms even go viral and begin to affect the reality many people experience. We pick up these transmissions all the time.

Thankfully with the power to create also comes the power to destroy. We can dissolve any thought-form we think doesn't serve us. We can empower the thought-forms that support our highest good. We can use a thought-form we created to also read the energy of a situation or person. For this meditation, have something you want to create in your life and something you want more information about in mind.

Meditation of Creativity

Hold the seventeenth bead of your blessing cord, the bead of creativity, the bead of Fire in Netzach.

Count yourself down into a meditative state.

Allow the screen of your mind to expand until it is a sphere around you. Feel the sensation of rising as a green light begins to fill the sphere. Resonate the god name of Netzach: *Yod-heh-vau-Heh Tza-ba-oth.*

The green light surrounds you and becomes a mist. As the green mist begins to fade, you find yourself in a garden. This garden is an interface for you to see your thought-forms and interact with them. Look around your garden.

Observe what it looks like. Everything here is a symbol for the thought-forms you have been putting into your energy field. Everything here is your creation, the garden you have planted and tended.

Does anything in the garden displease you or feel wrong to you? It could be represented by weeds, boulders, ugly clown statues, or anything that seems like it is out of place. Move toward this symbol and, if you can, touch it. Be open to what it has to tell you about itself. You may perceive this information in different ways. Sometimes the symbol will talk all by itself. What does it represent? Do you want to continue being affected by this thought-form? If not, begin to destroy it or transform it. For weeds, that would mean pulling them up and putting them on the compost pile. For boulders, try moving, hammering, or chiseling them down and using them to line the garden. Break up the clown statues into a new mosaic. Any way you want to transform this energy into something new is valid.

If you don't think changing its shape is enough, remember in this place you are in complete control of your reality. By your will alone, you can make unwanted things explode or dissolve, returning them into the energies from which they were formed. Try it on one of the symbols in your garden. When you destroy or change something in this garden, you are freeing up energies that can be used to create new things or feed what you truly want.

Now think of a situation or person you want to know more about or at least get a read on. Create a clear crystal symbol to use as a reading interface. It can be a crystal rose or a crystal garden ball. Let this thought-form be free and pure of any energies that might bias the reading. Then call some of the energy of the situation or person into the crystal. You will see an immediate change in the symbol. Note what color it becomes, how it feels to you now, any images that come to mind when you gaze at your symbol. Sometimes the crystal or rose will change in appearance. Roses may grow roots, make more blooms, or even start to burn. Any reaction can be interpreted as information about that person or situation. You can even talk to the symbol to get information. When you feel you have gotten all the information you are going to get, destroy the symbol, freeing up the energy to return to whence it came.

Now find a free space in your garden to create something new in you life. It can be anything you desire, even a quality. With your will, create a seed or seedling that represents your new creation in your life. Plant this into the soil of your mind. Give it the water and attention that it needs to thrive. Access the energy around you and give some energy and power to your new creation. Then walk away from it to the place where you became aware of the garden around you.

Green light begins to fill the garden again, obscuring it from view. The green begins to fade as you feel a gentle descent. The screen of your mind begins to return to its normal size.

Count yourself up into waking consciousness.

Give yourself clearance and balance. Ground and center yourself as needed. Write down your experience.

The Blessing Cord

Contemplation

What are you creating right now? What is on the "altar of your mind"? What project is it time to let go of so you can have more energy to create what you truly desire? What clutters up your physical and psychic space that could be removed? Think about how every creation is an act of destruction and every act of destruction is an act of creation.

DARING

The eighteenth bead of the blessing cord is the blessing of daring. It is the blessing of Fire in Hod, daring yourself to move past fear to do the things that you truly desire to do. One of the spiritual teachings often referred to as the Magician's Pyramid, Witches' Pyramid, or the Four Powers of the Sphinx says great magicians should have four things: they must seek to know, to will, to be silent—and to dare. No act of magic can be made without daring to wish for what you want.

In a recent Introduction to Witchcraft class, I was teaching the art of petition spells in a group. Each student had to come up with something they wanted to create within their lives and put it into a petition so they could read it aloud and add the group's energy and support to their spell. It was amazing how difficult this could be to those new to the path of magick. In our discussion of our spells, they said how vulnerable they felt saying what it was they wanted in front of others, how it was hard to ask for the things they personally wanted, and how they feared doing the spell wrong. Each one dared to get past these feelings, to put forth a call to what it was they needed. I was reminded of how much magick there is in just the act of daring to cast a spell for what you want and need.

The blockage of fear is challenged by the power of daring and courage. Fear can hold us back from achieving our dreams. Fear can scare us into thinking we shouldn't ask for what it is we want because we might sound selfish or be judged as weak for needing a desire fulfilled. Fear is an emotion that has helped us to avoid danger and that is why it can be so addictive.

There is an old joke where a guy walks by another guy spraying something in the air. The first guy asks, "What are you doing?" The second guy says, "Spraying anti-elephant spray!" The first guy says, "Really? How do you know it works?" The other guy says, "You haven't seen any elephants around, have you?" This shows us how fear can become a ritual. We are afraid of leaving the normal and everyday rituals of life because we are afraid of the catastrophes that could happen, so afraid we buy into the anti-elephant spray of beliefs built on fear because by sticking to that practice, we never see any elephants—or the results we don't want. We may never see these "elephants": we just fear that without our anti-elephant spray, we will.

We have to confront these fears that stop us and see if they are truly well-founded. We must dare to challenge them if we are to grow as individuals. Think of something you have always been afraid to do, something that is good for you but you could "never dare" to do. In this meditation we will confront a fear and find the heart of its truth.

Meditation of Daring

Hold the eighteenth bead of the blessing cord, the bead of daring, the blessing of Fire in Hod.

Count yourself down into a meditative state.

The Blessing Cord

Allow the screen of your mind to expand until it is a sphere around you. Feel a sensation of rising as your sphere begins to fill with an orange light. Resonate the god name *El-oh-heem Tza-ba-oth*.

Feel the mercurial orange light rise around you like mist. In the mist before you, call forth your Sword of Truth. It appears before you. Take up the sword. Feel its weight in your spiritual hand. Know that this sword has the power to reveal the truth of any situation. All you have to do is point it at a being and command it to reveal its truth. Connect with the power of the sword.

Call out to the fears that hold you back from doing what you most want to do. Command them to take form before you. They may look like spirits, a situation played out before you, demons, shadows, or any other myriad nasties. Look upon the form and shape of your fear and observe it dispassionately.

Point your Sword of Truth at an aspect of your fear. Ask for its name and aspect. It may give you a name to call it and tell you what kind of fear it is. If it does not, ask it again with the sword. If this doesn't work, ask one more time. If it doesn't answer, tell it that it cannot be a real fear if it can't be named and banish it.

If it names itself, ask if that is its true name. It may give you another name. Keep asking until it is a name of a fear that rings true. Fears can have many layers. Command this fear by its name to show you its root cause. What created this fear in your life? You may see a scene with a parent, a bad school experience, or even something that happened to you in another life. Experience the vision of this root cause.

Using the Sword of Truth, point at this vision and say that you understand the creation of this fear and it now no longer serves you. Draw an X over the fear and say, "I dissolve, neutralize, and banish this fear. It no longer has power over me." The being of fear begins to fade and dissolve from view as you neutralize its root cause, as if it were unraveling.

Hold your Sword of Truth before you in vision and say a statement of affirmation about doing the thing you were held back from by fear for so long. An example would be: "I dare to be a freelance artist! I dare to find a fulfilling job" and so forth. You may hear a ringing or singing from your Sword of Truth if this has become your new truth.

Thank the Sword of Truth and allow it to return to its rightful place until you need it again.

Feel a gentle descent as the light begins to fade from your sphere. The screen of your mind returns to normal coloring and then shrinks back to normal size.

Count yourself up to waking consciousness.

Give yourself clearance and balance. Ground and center as needed. Write down your experiences.

Contemplation

Give thought to how fear has held you back in the past. What requires daring in your life if you are to achieve it? Is there anything that is really stopping you from doing what it is you love? If so, what is it and why?

CLARITY

The nineteenth bead of the blessing cord is the blessing of clarity, the blessing Fire in Yesod. The sphere of the Moon is so aligned with the element of water, it is difficult to think of it having a power of fire. I think of the fire of this sphere like the light of the Moon: reflected light of the "vision" of the solar sphere of Tiphereth. In this sphere we can use the power of the Moon to reflect and gain clarity on anything that needs it.

Yesod is associated with the astral realm and the wellspring of all thoughts and images that have ever been. It is the place where psychic information is paired with image and emotion. In this sphere, we can scry to a greater effect than we can here in the physical world of Malkuth. The images and insights we get from scrying in Yesod come clearer here because the images and symbols that give us information during scrying originate from here.

Scrying is the art of using a reflective surface to gain psychic information. We have all seen the images of the psychic or fortune-teller looking into a crystal ball to see the future. Scrying was the method used by many psychics and magicians to gain insight and prophecy. Nostradamus was said to use a bowl of water to obtain all his prophesies. John Dee and Edward Kelly used a crystal ball and an obsidian mirror to scry and communicate with angels. In this meditation, we go to the pool of the Moon to scry out answers, seeking clarity around an issue. As I said before, it is easier to scry in the astral, so this is an interesting experience. I have used it to help interpret dreams, gain ideas, or just to answer questions.

Meditation of Clarity

Hold the nineteenth bead of the blessing cord, the bead of clarity, the blessing of Air in Yesod.

Count yourself down into a meditative state.

Allow the screen of your mind to expand until it is a sphere around you. Feel a sensation of rising as your sphere begins to fill with a purple misty light. Resonate the god name of Yesod: *Sha-dai El-chai.*

The purple light begins to fade and before you is the opening to a grotto. The night sky above you is filled with stars and a bright Full Moon. As you step into the the cave, you see that inside there is a still pool of water at its center. Above the pool there is an opening in the ceiling where moonlight streams down. The Moon's light reflects upon the water. The wind begins to stir over the water, making nets of light ripple and dance across its surface and the walls of the cave.

Come closer to the pool of water. Get comfortable beside this beautiful pool. Fill your mind with the aspects of your question as you gaze at the pool. See the rippling light dance. When you feel you have expressed your question with your mind, say it aloud to yourself in this place. When you have voiced your question, allow your mind to clear. Take deep, slow breaths, releasing any thoughts about the situation. Allow the pool's reflected light to smooth away all thoughts about the question until you are open.

When your mind is clear and receptive, you may start to see shapes or images in the pool. Just observe them and allow them to come to you. You may perceive thoughts or feelings or hear words. Be open to the experience and try to remain in the neutral open-minded state. Allow the information to come without judgement. You can recount this later for your own interpretation.

When the images stop, your answer seems clear, or you feel like you are done, begin to stand up next to the moonlit pool. Thank this space for its wisdom and clarity. Step back through the entrance to the cave. The purple light begins to rise, obscuring your view of the cave, and you feel a gentle descent. The purple light fades. The screen of your mind becomes its normal color and shrinks back to its normal size.

Count yourself up into waking consciousness.

Give yourself clearance and balance. Ground and center as needed. Write down your experiences.

Contemplation:

What do you need clarity around? What can you move forward on now that you have this clarity? Do you sometimes get stuck in your search for clarity and not move forward with something? Psychic work is well and good, but sometimes we just have to move forward and do something in order to get the clarity of success or failure.

INCARNATE SPIRIT

The twentieth bead in the blessing cord is the blessing of incarnate spirit. This is the Fire of Malkuth. The earthy sphere of Malkuth could not move and live without the spirit which animates it. Every flower, every animal, every human being is a part of the Great Spirit that has inhabited a body to have an earthly experience. Each one of us is an incarnate spirit that has come into this world for a reason. Some of us have done this many times, if you believe in reincarnation. We emerged from the well of souls and returned to the earthly plane to learn, to grow, to experience and, at the end of our lives, return to that well to share our experience with the Great Spirit.

If you are reading this book, you have chosen to become an incarnate spirit for this time. This gives you different options on how you can affect the world than, say, a spirit guide.

I was asked by one of my students recently why spirit guides would want to work with us. Spirit guides want to work with us because we can affect this world. We have more power in the world than they can easily manifest. We can tap into the very soul and nature of this world, which spirits have a lesser ability to do. Just as spirit guides can channel energies from spiritual realms to us, we can in turn channel physical plane energies to them to use for their benefit. We are spirits just like them, with our own access to wisdom of bodily experience.

A powerful technique is to work in concert with these spiritual guides, mixing spiritual energies with the material energies of nature. When we run energies with a spirit guide, we can build up power to make changes in our lives.

Meditation of Incarnate Spirit

Hold the twentieth bead on the blessing cord, the blessing of incarnate spirit, the bead of Fire in Malkuth.

Count yourself down into a meditative state.

Allow the screen of your mind to expand around you, forming a sphere. Feel the slight shift as a garden begins to grow up around you in the sphere of your mind. Resonate the god name of Malkuth: *Ah-do-nai Ha-ah-retz.*

Explore the garden of Malkuth. Take off your spiritual footwear (if any) and allow your feet to connect to the earth. As they touch the earth, you can feel the energies of all that is manifest around you. Allow the energy centers in your feet to open gently and begin to cycle this energy of the manifest world. The earth's energy begins to flow up your legs. Into your pelvic bowl. Up into your belly. Rising into your chest. Overflowing into your arms and up into your head. Filling your body with this manifest energy.

Put out the mental call to your spirit guides. See them come into the garden. Ask one of them to exchange energy with you to show you the reciprocal nature of the energies of spirit and the energies of the manifest. Choose a guide you trust and have worked with before. As your guide comes before you, one of their hands (if they have them) begins to form a ball of energy around it made of the highest spiritual vibrations. This is the energy the spirits use to make changes on the spiritual levels.

Like them, you raise your hand, and a pulsing ball of manifest energy comes into being around your hand. Your guide reaches out with their other hand, then the hand with the energy to touch your hand with the energy. You reach out with your other hand and touch their hand with the energy.

Once you have both connected, the energy begins to flow in a circuit between you and your connected hands. You feel the pure energy of the spirit world flowing into you and the material energy flowing out of you into your guide and then back around. The energies begin to blend. Feel the power you are sharing with your guide and your guide is sharing with you. The longer you hold it, the more intense it feels.

When you and your guide feel like you have built up enough energy, let your hands release and send the energy out like a shower above you both. This technique can be used to raise energy to be sent out for a desired change. For your first time, just feel the release, without any focused intention.

Thank your guide for their aid. They may also thank you for the experience.

Return to where you entered the garden. Become aware of the garden around you in your sphere. Allow it to fade as you feel a slight shift. Your screen of your mind returns to its normal size.

Count yourself up into waking consciousness.

Give yourself clearance and balance. Ground and center as needed. Write down your experience.

Contemplation

Why did you incarnate? Why do you think spirit guides want to work with us? What advantages do you offer to the spirits and what advantages do they offer you in partnership?

INTUITION

The twenty-first bead in the blessing cord starts a new elemental cycle of water. The blessing of this bead is intuition, the blessing of Water of Kether. Our intuition is always with us. We all have it to a variety of degrees, and there are a multitude of ways it can come to us. We may feel, see, remember, dream, hear, know, smell, or taste our intuition speaking to us. Many of us can get hung up on how our intuition speaks to us, but it can be different every time. It is always trying to speak to us. Our own filters of reality, beliefs, fears, and reactions can block out this ever-present gentle prodding from spiritual guidance.

Our upbringing can block our intuition by giving us patterns that don't let us connect to a greater source. You may have gotten a wild idea as a kid, and then your parents shut down this intuitive burst with their own fears. Don't blame them, though; they are just the current link in a chain of family and culture that taught children not to listen to intuition. Thankfully we are our own people and can choose to change these beliefs and fears.

What I think is the hardest part of intuition is to "hear" it and to trust it. To hear it we must quiet the louder parts of ourselves: fears, beliefs, and our own doubting self all have loud voices in our minds. Stilling these can be done with passive meditation or by focusing on your breathing until your mind becomes still. This is when our intuition can speak clearly, but we don't always need to be in this state to hear it. Just by thinking about a situation, focusing our attention lightly on it, and clearing our mind momentarily so we can receive intuitive signal is enough. The first thought, image, feeling, or memory—or other sensory input—is our answer.

The second part is to trust it. Some wild and strange things can come through the intuition. Sometimes it skips forward to the end steps, and you find it hard to see how it got there. The important thing is that you trust it. You can start small by listening to your intuition and following its guidance on small issues. This builds your confidence in your intuitive connection. The more we trust our intuition and psychic guidance, the more of it we seem to have. Our lives begin to feel more alive when we follow our intuition. Things seem brighter, and people start to wonder where you got the ideas from.

In the following meditation, we use an interface called the tube of intuitive flow so we can clear our intuitive flow of any blockages like beliefs, fears, or reactions. This meditation shows us we can connect with our intuition and ask it anything about itself and receive intuitive answers. We can follow these answers to clear our energetic connection with our guides and spirits. The clearer we are, the stronger the "voice" of our intuition is.

Meditation of Intuition

Hold the twenty-first bead of the blessing cord, the bead of intuition, the Water of Kether.

Count yourself down into a meditative state.

Visualize the screen of your mind expanding into a sphere around you. You feel a sense of rising as your sphere begins to fill with radiant prismatic light. Resonate the god name of Kether: *Eh-heh-e-yeh.*

When the light clears, you see above you a spherical shape made of whirling light. This sphere is the divine source of intuition. You may see within it guides, radiant energies, and sometimes passing images. Ask to conjure your channel of intuition from the radiant source. See it as a tube that comes down from the source and passes through your crown and all the way down the trunk of your body, down into the center of the earth. This tube is an interface with your stream of intuition. Send your thoughts inside the tube to observe its interior.

Inside the tube, you may see clumps or clots, places where your stream of intuition is blocked in some way. Each of these blocks slows your intuition or can even dam up its flow. You have the power of intuition and can reach out to connect to these blocks and speak with them. Choose a blockage and mentally connect with it. Ask it what fear or belief created it. The blockage will give you a memory, an image, words, a feeling, or just a sense of knowing about how it started in the first place. Know that this is your energy speaking to you. You have the power to use your awareness to change it. Let the blockage tell you how it started. Then ask what intuitive action you need to take to change it. The blockage may give you instructions. You may need to forgive someone, change a thought process you have, do something daring, trust your intuition to help you. Once you know what it is the blockage needs to change, ask it if you can help it clear energetically right now. If yes, place it between your two mental hands. Imagine white light flowing from your hands and dissolving the blockage. Any stagnant energy will naturally flow down the tube to your place of grounding at its end. You may feel lighter. You may have more intuitive flashes without this blockage. Seek to trust your impressions.

You can continue this exercise with each blockage you find or end it now and return to this conjured tube that contains your flow later to clear it more. When you are done, move your consciousness out of the tube. Imagine your awareness of it fading, knowing it is just a symbolic interface of your intuitive flow. See the source of your intuition above you and give it thanks for its guidance as it fades from view.

The scene begins to obscure as prismatic white light fills the sphere again. You feel a gentle descent as the sphere again returns to normal color. It shrinks back to its normal size as the screen of your mind again.

Count yourself up into waking consciousness.

Give yourself clearance and balance. Ground and center as needed. Write down your experience.

Contemplation

Throughout the day connect with your intuition by asking yourself what you sense about your daily situations. Do you recognize your intuition when it "speaks" to you? What holds you back from sensing your intuition? Do you trust your intuition? If not, why?

The Blessing Cord

FLOW

The twenty-second bead in the blessing cord has the blessing of flow. This is the blessing of Water in Chokhmah. Chokmah always adds motion and movement to the elements it affects. In air, it is the movement of the word, and in fire, it is the movement of doing our will. When it comes to water, it is flow. Flow is the currents and tides of our surroundings. It can be the stillness of stagnation or the rushing flow of too much activity. This can be on many levels of reality: energetic, emotional, physical, mental—all have a tide and flow to them. This can be affected by astrology, the surroundings, geopathic stress, group-minds, and even your own personal flow.

When I was a kid, we had a big round pool in our backyard. My friends and I would make a whirlpool in it by starting to swim around the pool in a circle until the water began to move with us. Our flow began to change the flow of the pool. Then we would all let go and float and let the flow we created carry us around the pool. Sometimes we would all try to go against the flow to test our strength. In this smaller environment of the pool, we had enough flow to change the overall flow. In the ocean of life, we would need a lot more energy to change the flow.

When a coven works together to make a cone of power, it is much like this example of the pool. If the coven is using dance to raise energy, they dance around the circle faster and faster making a sort of whirlpool within the "pool" of their circle. When the energy gets moving, it is easier to feel and direct than stagnant energy. Much like air, you can feel it more when it is moving, like the wind. This movement of energy in circle is the way we increase the intensity and purity of the energy.

If we want to engage the flow around us, we first have to be aware of where it is going. This is where we connect to what we can feel and intuit about the flow of energy. Sometimes the current of flow is so big it is hard to tell where it is flowing. Like when you get caught up in an ocean current. Being aware of the energies in your area can help, like knowing where places of power and ley lines are. It can also be helpful to know the effects of planetary energies going on because this can affect the flow. When it comes to magick, the Moon's cycle can affect the flow. Knowing the effect of a flow may involve just going along with it to explore where it goes. We don't always know. Let your intuition be your guide. Connect to the flow around you and ask it where it is going.

Once you have awareness, you can choose to go with the flow or go against the flow. Both have good points. When the flow is going in a direction you want to go in, you can use that flow to surf or swim yourself towards what it is you want. You can enhance your efforts by going with the flow to get to your next destination or manifestation faster. It takes less energy to go with the flow than against it. If the flow is not taking you where you want to go or you need to build some strength, going against the flow is an option. Going against the flow takes more energy, yet can be rewarding because you become stronger personally. The next time the flow goes your way, you will be stronger because you had the discipline to go against it when it didn't. The last option is to use the flow to get out of the current. By moving at an angle—neither with or against—you use a little of the flow and your own strength to get you to a place where you have more control of your motion.

Meditation of Flow

Hold the twenty-second bead on the blessing cord, the bead of flow, the blessing of Water in Chokmah.

Count yourself down into a meditative state.

Allow the screen of your mind to expand around you to form a sphere. Resonate the god name of Chokmah: *Yod heh vauv Heh.*

You feel a rising feeling as the sphere begins to fill with gray misty light all around you. The mist begins to clear and in front of you is an estuary. You can see the small bay of sea water all the way to the other side as the mist clears.

Beside you are three floating lanterns ready to go into the water. Throw the first out into the water. This one gets caught by the current immediately and begins to move around the estuary. The current takes it quickly around the small bay and out into the ocean.

Throw the second lantern out a little further. This one moves a bit slower as it goes around the middle of the current and out into the ocean.

Throw the third lantern into the middle of the estuary. This one just swirls around the middle of the small bay. Now that you know the estuary's flow, it is time to feel it for yourself. Step into the water and feel the flow. The current is strong and moves around your body. Allow the flow to move you as you float. Feel the effortless movement as you engage the flow.

Now try to swim with the flow. See how fast you can move when you are going with the flow and adding your energy to it. Enjoy the speed and rush of movement.

Now try to swim against the flow. Feel your strength. See how your efforts stop you in motion or reverse your motion. The more you work against the flow, the stronger you become.

Now shift yourself to swim at an angle to the flow so you can move into the center of the estuary where the last lantern is still circling around. Here you can feel the flow swirling around you. Move again at an angle to slip back into the flow before where you started swimming. Allow the flow to bring you back to the shore where you started.

As you sit on the shore, reflect on your experience. What are you doing now, going with the flow, going against the flow, or swimming for the center where you can plan where you will engage the flow? This is just a metaphor for tapping into the energies around you. Take this knowledge with you. Become aware of the flow around you and choose how to respond appropriately.

The gray mists rise up around you, filling your sphere. Feel a gentle descent as it begins to fade and your sphere becomes its normal color. Allow the screen of your mind to return to its normal size.

Count yourself up into waking consciousness.

Give yourself clearance and balance. Ground and center as needed. Write down your experiences.

The Blessing Cord

Contemplation.

Where is the flow around you going? When you connect to the flow, what does it tell you about itself? What is your choice of how to respond? How can you use awareness of flow to enhance your life?

SURRENDER

The twenty-third bead in the blessing cord is the blessing of surrender. This is the blessing of Water in Binah. When we talk about surrender, it always makes me think of cowboys raising a white flag of truce made out of someone's knickers tied to a stick. This surrender is not the one we are talking about, however. When I say "surrender," it refers to surrender to the Great Spirit's direction and flow.

In the previous blessing of flow, we recognized where the flow was taking us and chose to go with it or against it, one way or another. In surrender, we open up to the Great Spirit's flow, opening up and letting the flow of spirit move through us and guide us. We surrender control and expectation. We accept the divine's energy and blessings, trusting them to lead us where we need to be.

When we hold too tightly to what we want to be or to an idea, we can strangle the energy for its growth. The energy of spirit can be much like water through a hose: If you hold the hose too tightly or pinch it off, the water can't flow. We have to surrender our tight hold to let the water flow, as it needs to.

In the Wheel of Time series of novels by Robert Jordan and Brandon Sanderson, there are two ways to connect to the One Power that is the source of the magic in their fantasy world: one for the male side of this force and one for the female side. The male side enters a visionary void where there is nothing but a flame in the center, representing the male side of the One Power. The void brings detachment, but also awareness. They reach out and grab the flame in the center, and the more forcefully they grab it, the more energy they can fill themselves with. The detached awareness they gain from the void is their surrender. They let go of all attachment and feeling to grab their source. The feminine way to get energy from this source is to visualize they are a flower with their source above them. Their flower relaxes and opens up to the source, drawing in that energy and letting it flow through them. Their relaxation and openness to this source of power is their surrender to this energy. This fantasy series gives two great—and different—examples of how to surrender to gain energy and wisdom. I have personally used both in meditation and found them both to be interesting exercises. They inspired my meditation of surrender.

Meditation of Surrender

Hold the twenty-third bead of the blessing cord, the bead of the Water of Binah, the bead of surrender.

Count yourself down into a meditative state.

Allow the screen of your mind to expand to create a sphere around you. Feel a rising sensation as the sphere begins to lose all illumination, until you are surrounded by a black endless void. Resonate the god name of Binah: *Yod Heh Vauv Heh El-oh-heem.*

Allow yourself to relax deeper as you float in the inky void. You are weightless here, as if you were in the depths of space. Surrender any tension or thoughts to the void. Allow any emotions to dissipate into the void. Release your expectations and find the peace of detachment that comes from the void.

A brilliant star of light bursts into life within the void. This star is a representation of the Great Spirit. You can feel it calling to you. As its light hits your crown, a beautiful flower blooms within your head. Surrender all as you open up to the Great Spirit. Your mind clears even more as you open, as you connect to this infinite light.

As this bloom begins to open, another blossom opens in the center of your chest at your heart area. It opens and drinks in the light of spirit. You may feel a sensation of bliss that comes from surrendering to spirit. Your heart grows lighter the more it opens.

A bloom opens at your pelvic bowl's root, right where your body meets a chair. As this flower opens, you surrender any tension as a wave of healing strength flows from spirit into this flower. As you surrender, the light flows into this bloom, and from this bloom the light spreads to your whole body. Relax and surrender to the energy of the Great Spirit.

At this point, open to any messages spirit might have for you. Surrender and accept what comes, whether in voice, vision, or knowledge. When you feel like you are ready, send a breath of gratitude up toward the Great Spirit.

The void and star begin to fade as you feel a gentle descent. Know that this place is always there when you need it. Your screen returns to its normal shape and size.

Count yourself back up to waking consciousness.

Give yourself clearance and balance. Ground and center as needed. Write down your experience.

Contemplation

What do you need in order to surrender and be open to the plans of the Great Spirit? What are you holding too tightly? Now that you know what the connection to spirit feels like, review some of your choices: Do they make you feel alive and filled with the divine or do they feel diminishing and constraining?

COMPASSION

The twenty-fourth bead on the blessing cord is the blessing of compassion. It is the blessing of Water in Chesed. Chesed is the sphere of Mercy. Its vibration is one of care and concern, but it also sees the bigger picture better than some of the other spheres.

Compassion means "to suffer with." This can spur many forms of response depending on our nature. It is hard to suffer along with someone, to feel empathy for what is going on with someone, knowing that you can do little to help. Part of life is suffering, and most of us create more for ourselves by becoming too attached to our wants.

I have found in my own path through life that my best expressions of compassion for others come when I am not attached to a certain outcome. I have had students in the past where I would observe their struggles with what I thought was compassion and then offer them advice and assistance, only to see them manifest mental blocks and excuses to why all my advice would not work and then tell me I was egotistical to think I could help. Sometimes my offers were met by flat-out refusal, and in some cases, a loss of friendship. I came to realize people both want and need to solve things for themselves, and they are not always in the place to do so. I had become attached to the outcome of my friends' success without letting them process the suffering and come to their own answers.

Now I hold compassion for where people are in the present. I ask questions to get clarity about what it is they are experiencing, so I can hold compassion for them where they are. I ask them if they want advice and then release any attachment to them actually doing what I said. Compassionately I know that they must find their own way. It is a hard stance to have knowing that I want them to do well.

Our world can seem filled with endless suffering: prejudice, privilege, poverty, hunger, despair, our political climate, our world climate, fear, xenophobia, and much, much more. Watch the nightly news for a while, and you will see the harsh suffering in the world. It can make us feel powerless. Don't believe the hype. You can make a difference. You can be the change you wish to see in the world.

This meditation is inspired by the Buddhist practice called heart breathing. We breathe in some of the suffering of the world and transform it into peace and love. This practice is a tough one and should not become a daily practice for anyone. It is emotionally draining and can affect your health after a while. This is why in this meditation, you are led to cleanse both before and after and are set in a place where you can be distant from the suffering of the world so you can have compassion without attachment.

Meditation of Compassion

Hold the twenty-forth bead of your blessing cord, the bead of compassion, the bead of the blessing of Water in Chesed.

The Blessing Cord

Count yourself down into a meditative state.

Allow the screen of your mind to expand to create a sphere around you. Feel a rising sensation as sky-blue or electric blue light begins to fill the sphere. Resonate the god name of Chesed: *El.*

A blue cloud seems to form around your feet. It is strangely solid, and you can stand upon it. As the light begins to fade, you see that you are high above the world on a blue cloud. From this place you can see the bigger picture of the world. Look up into the endless blue of the sky. Start to breathe this blue light of the sky into yourself. As you breathe out, release your tension and worry. Breathe in this light and feel yourself filling with cleansing energy. It begins to transform your energy, making your vibration stronger. It builds until you are filled with light.

Now feel your heart begin to open like a swirling vortex of light. You notice it growing large as it fills with compassion. There is an endless flow of this compassion and peace. Focus on the world below you. Breathe in some of the suffering of the world, filling your lungs fully. Hold the breath as it mixes with and transforms in your vortex of the heart. Release your breath, imagining yourself breathing out peace, harmony, and compassion.

Breathe in again the suffering of the world for the count of seven. Hold and let this energy transform within you for the count of seven. Breathe out peace, compassion, and harmony back into the world. Do this about five more times or until you think you have had enough. Breathe in the suffering on your last breath, hold and transform, and breathe the energy up to the gods in a prayer of peace and compassion for all.

Begin to breathe in the light of the sky and breathe out anything that doesn't serve, releasing it. Keep doing this breathing practice until you feel clear and balanced again.

Allow the blue light to return, obscuring your view of the sky, world, and cloud. As the light dims again, feel a gentle descent. Your screen returns to its normal size.

Count yourself up into normal consciousness.

Give yourself clearance and balance. Ground and center yourself as needed. Write down your experience.

Contemplation

Is there a difference between compassion and pity? When you are hardest on yourself, can you turn that into compassion for yourself where you are? Have you had compassion for the people in your life without attachment to their success or failure, just unconditionally giving them compassion?

RELEASE

The twenty-fifth bead in the blessing cord is the blessing of release. It is the Water of Geburah. Geburah has great power but also brings hard lessons. The lesson and blessing it brings is release. Release needs to happen for us to have clear, flowing connection to spirit and our own life path. Sometimes it is a pattern we have been consciously engaging in that we need to let go of so we can move forward. It might be something left over from our parents or a past life. It can even be something we manifested that is no longer good for us, like the junk in our house or a job that is no longer working for us.

In the Craft, we use the Waxing Moon to grow things and the Waning Moon to dissolve and banish. We get all excited during the Waxing Moon to start new things and make new manifestations. One of the best pieces of advice I have ever gotten was to make room for these new things in my mind, in my heart, and in my home, during the Waning Moon. The older I get, the more I see this as true. I now know that I need to prioritize what I keep and hold on to. I have created a lot, and I have to be able to let some of the things I have collected go, whether they are destroyed or moved on to a place where they can be loved.

This process can be hard. Ask yourself: Does this still serve me? Does it bring me joy? Does this help me along my path? Evaluate if this is something you still need. If not, it is time for release. Make some room for new manifestations.

In our minds we may have patterns we need to release to be able to move forward into the world we want. These old patterns can still be creating the things we don't want in life and draining some of our energy or blocking our flow. Sometimes just making a list of what our limiting beliefs or patterns are can help us in this process. Get a piece of paper and write on it: "The reason I can't have (your goal) is because..." Set a timer for two minutes and write down every reason that comes to mind about why you can't have your goal. When the bell goes off, stop and look at your list. These are the patterns you are going to have to clear away to help your manifestation come into being. Do the meditation of release and then rip up this list.

Meditation of Release

Hold the twenty-fifth bead, the bead of the blessing of release, the blessing of Water in Geburah.

Count yourself down into a meditative state.

Allow the screen of your mind to expand to create a sphere around you. Feel a rising sensation as the sphere fills with a red light. Vibrate the god name of Geburah: *El-oh-heem Gi-boor*.

The red light fills you with the power to release. As the light clears, you are in a place that represents your mind. This could be a large garden, a house, a castle, or any place that resonates with you. This is your special place. You have full control of your environment. Focus your thoughts on the first belief on your list. Follow your intuition to the place where this belief lives. It will have a symbolic representation in your inner space. Once you have found it,

The Blessing Cord

observe how it is reacting to the things around it. How does it affect your place? Touch it and ask to see when this thing was created. Why did it serve you then? Does it serve you now?

Begin to change the belief. In a garden of the mind, this may mean weeding it out. In the attic of the mind, it may mean cleaning it out to be dumped or burning it in the mental yard outside. In the castle, you might want to put it in a catapult and shoot it outside. The solutions to changing this symbol of your old belief are infinite. Choose one that works for you.

You can now repeat the process with all the beliefs on your list. When you are done, experience how clear you feel. In a later meditation, plant or create some new beliefs that move you toward your goals.

The red light begins to fill your sphere again, blotting out the grove. You feel a gentle descent as the red light fades. Your sphere returns to the shape and size of the screen of the mind.

Count yourself up into waking consciousness.

Give yourself clearance and balance. Ground and center yourself as needed. Write down your experience.

Contemplation

Look around your home and begin to release the things that are cluttering your energy. Ask yourself: does this bring me joy? Does this serve a purpose? Is this in alignment with my Great Work? If it is not, why keep it at all? Observe your mind. Are there patterns you could release to have a better flow and clearer mind?

FORGIVENESS

The twenty-sixth bead in the blessing cord is the blessing of forgiveness, the Water of Tiphereth. I admit, as a pagan, forgiveness felt alien to me. It always felt like a Christian concept that had nothing to do with being spiritual and more to do with being a martyr. It wasn't until I heard that forgiveness isn't for the other person, that it was really for you, that it made sense to me.

We unconsciously hold the energy of disagreements and betrayals between people. Our soul's path becomes strongly linked to the anger, hate, and resentment we feel for a person. This energy is another thing that can block our flow to manifesting what it is we are truly here to do. We don't have to forget what someone has done. We don't even have to let that person back into our lives. By forgiving them, we let go of how they affect us.

If you had the flu last year and got it treated and now you are fine, do you still feel the sickness? No, you may remember the sickness, but you don't feel it any more. This is how you want to be with forgiveness. You can remember what was done, but it no longer holds any emotional charge for you. A good test to see if you have really forgiven someone is to imagine another person telling you how great they are doing now and how they have everything they want. If you feel any pain or anger, you haven't fully forgiven them.

When you forgive and let go of this energy you're holding, both your lives will improve. When I have done the meditation that follows, I have felt lighter every time. When we forgive, we make room for newer and happier circumstances, as we discovered in our work of releasing with the previous bead.

Before this meditation, you may want to list all the people you think have done you wrong in some way and memorize the release statement.

Meditation of Forgiveness

Hold the twenty-sixth bead, the bead of the blessing of forgiveness, the blessing of Water in Tiphereth.

Count yourself down into a meditative state.

Allow the screen of your mind to expand into a sphere around you. Feel a rising sensation as your sphere begins to fill with radiant golden yellow light. Vibrate the god name of Tiphereth: *Yod-heh-vauv-heh el-oh-ah Vah-dah-ath.*

The light fades, and you are in a golden field. Above you is a golden white sphere that represents the highest and best of the universe. Within it you might see Goddess, God, Great Spirit, your guides, or your higher self. It is the highest guidance and power. Thank it for its presence in this work and ask for its aid.

Conjure the people you have to forgive. You can do this by calling up a person who is on your list or just calling out to someone you need to forgive. They appear in the field. Tell them what they did that you are trying to forgive.

Then say the following statement of release and forgiveness with all of your being:

The Blessing Cord

"(Their name), I forgive you for your imperfections as I forgive myself for mine. I release (what you are feeling) I have against you. I forgive and release you to be who you are and to be happy. I release you to be free. With that I am free."

After you feel it has done its work, the person begins to rise in the air to the ball of golden white light above you. As they float away, you are releasing them to the universe. You can then repeat the process with others on your list.

When you are done, say to yourself in this place of power: "I forgive and release you all, as I forgive myself for all. Blessed be!"

Golden light again begins to fill the area around you, making the world go opaque with the intensity of its glow. As the light fades, you feel a gentle descent. The screen of your mind begins to return to its normal size.

Count yourself up into waking consciousness.

Give yourself clearance and balance. Ground and center yourself as needed. Write down your experience.

Contemplation

Think about the people you have had to forgive: Is there a pattern to the story that manifests this pain? What are your contributions to this pattern? Can you forgive yourself? Can you forgive what was done to you? Can you release this pattern?

LOVE

The twenty-seventh bead in the blessing cord is the blessing of love. It is the blessing of Water in Netzach. In a first run-through of all the words I thought would be the focus of this book, I listed this one as "emotion" or "feeling." Though I think this is still true, when we begin to feel the emotions in this sphere, the heart of them all is love. This idea of the heart of emotions being love came from a vision in one of my meditations. In it, Aphrodite rose from the sea and grew to be crowned by the stars. She told me that the highest form of emotion was love. She went on to tell me how the power of love was what brought things together and separated them. I asked for more clarification, and she told me that love of others draws us together with others, and that love of self and experience separated us. She then went on to say that neither was better than the other, just different, and each was a part of our spiritual journey.

This made me think of the alchemical operations of separating and coming back together to create a more purified whole. The processes of alchemy are always about separating to purify and unifying to create something more potent. This is what Nature does at a slower rate, for she is the great alchemist. This thought of how love was both separating and joining astounded me as so intrinsic to the understanding of its force that I had to share it with you.

Aphrodite then reminded me of the comic *Promethea* and the journey of its characters to Netzach. The characters go into the waters of Netzach, and as they dive down, they experience a whole gamut of emotions. The deeper they go, the more they experience the knowledge and power of love, eventually coming face to face with Aphrodite herself and feeling divine love. Aphrodite wanted this to be the focus of this meditation: for people to feel the heart of love beneath the waves of consciousness.

I thanked her for her insight, and when I returned, I laughed about how it would be weeks before I was able to write this chapter. Aphrodite apparently wanted to get her request in early!

Meditation of Love

Hold the twenty-seventh bead of your blessing cord, the bead of love, the bead of Water in Netzach.

Count yourself down into a meditative state.

Allow the screen of your mind to expand until it is a sphere around you. Feel the sensation of rising as a green light begins to fill the sphere around you. Resonate the god name of Netzach: *Yod-heh-vau-Heh Tza-ba-oth.*

The green light surrounds you and becomes a mist. As the green mist begins to fade, you find yourself at the edge of a vast ocean. You can only see so far out into the ocean before there is green mist clouding the horizon. The water is a luminous green, as if it were lit from within by an underwater aurora borealis. You walk up to the edge of the water, and as soon as your feet and toes touch it, you can feel that this water is different. It is warm like bath water. When you touch it, you feel connected to it and everything, as though this ocean were more than ocean. This is the ocean of consciousness, a symbolic interface to the collective consciousness of all beings. You begin to walk forward deeper into the water. The delicious warmth of the water caresses you. As you get to chest level, you feel yourself taken by a gentle current, pulling you out into the ocean. It pulls you under, but strangely you can still breathe normally and easily.

As you float down deeper into the ocean, memories and emotions begin to flood up. You may see them reflected in the waters or in bubbles. Let these feelings flow and release them. Let the current carry you through them. They are your consciousness clearing old emotions so you can embrace what comes next more fully.

Deeper and deeper you go into this illuminated ocean, until you begin to see a brighter light coming closer and closer. This light takes the shape of Aphrodite, and as you draw closer, you can feel the love in the water. It blots out all other feelings. As you get closer, you see that Aphrodite is bigger than you thought. She is a giantess filled with love. As you come closer, she may give you a message or just allow you to look into her eyes and feel the enormity of her love for all. You feel your heart opening more than it has before, opening to love, and filling with it.

When you are ready, thank the goddess as the current pulls you back the way you came. As you rise, you notice the feelings you cleansed away don't return and don't have any effect on you. You are filled with the love of the goddess. Finally you break the surface near where you began and can feel the sand beneath your feet. You walk back onto the shore. As your feet leave the ocean, you can feel the separation, but you are full of love and know that you can connect and separate at will.

Green misty light fills the area, obscuring it from view. The green begins to fade as you feel a gentle descent. The screen of your mind returns to its normal size.

Count yourself up into waking consciousness.

Give yourself clearance and balance. Ground and center yourself as needed. Write down your experiences.

Contemplation.

What emotions do you feel when you think about love? There are many kinds of love; each one has conditions to it because we love ourselves. How has loving yourself separated you from others? Is this a bad thing? How has your love of others made you lose yourself in union? Is this a bad thing?

EXPRESSION

The twenty-eighth bead in the blessing cord is the blessing of expression. This blessing is the Water of Hod. Expression is the art of creating to convey our thoughts, feelings, spirit, and sometimes just our love of creating. In our world, we have a lot of reasons why people shouldn't express what they want or perceive. Social norms lead us away from making public spectacles of ourselves. We are told to be quiet, don't make a mess, and that our art isn't very good. Over time we begin to hear this outer voice in our heads coming from us.

I took an art therapy course in college, and I remember one of the continuing education students leaving the course. She was a talented musician, but when it came to art she didn't have any confidence in her skills. When confronted with the requirement of creating an art piece for class of her first memory, she couldn't even pick up the brush. She professed she had no skill at art and thought that she would be able to create music as her art therapy. The teacher said that wouldn't work for the confines of the class. The student became very upset because she just couldn't do art. She dropped the course before the next class. I always wondered how she became so closed off to all other types of expression but music. She and her children were all talented in music. I wondered that if she had only been encouraged to express herself as a youngster without judgment whether she would have been able to paint that memory. I wondered what the music she would have written for it would have sounded like.

Expression of our art is so important and powerful. In my later work, I found teaching kids to do art and encouraging any expression made them feel more confident. They were able to share what was on their minds and hearts more easily. They were calmer and happier because they could express what was inside. We just need a safe space where we can express those feelings. In this meditation we go to a place of expression and let loose our inner selves. I encourage you to express your experience in physical art by painting, drawing, making music, or whatever your art may be.

Meditation of Expression

Hold the twenty-eighth bead of the blessing cord, the bead of expression, the blessing of Water in Hod.

Count yourself down into a meditative state.

Allow the screen of your mind to expand until it is a sphere around you. Feel a sensation of rising as your sphere begins to fill with an orange light. Resonate the god name of Hod: *El-oh-heem Tza-ba-oth.*

Feel the mercurial orange light rise around you like mist. As the mist begins to clear, you are in a white room with no furnishings. All around you are blank walls. This a place that calls out for expression. In this place your mind and thoughts can paint whatever you please onto your room like a blank canvas.

The first step is to start to create your expression. You may want to splatter paint against the wall or make a detailed outline on the walls. It is up to you; it is your expression. Get into your expression and paint whatever you want to in this space. Get into the process of creating and really feel it. In the meditation you can fix any mistakes easily, but realize that any mistakes can lead your expression in a different way. Really get into the process because the process of expressing is part of the value of the experience.

Connect all your senses into your creation. Feel the paint, the clay, or whatever other medium you have chosen. What do you smell as you work? Feel the passion of expression. Claim this expression and love it just as it is. It is beautiful because it is yours. Express in this space fully with only the limitations that you choose. Here you can paint, sculpt, or do any art you want. This is your expression. Let your feelings flow out onto the walls of this room.

When you feel ready, observe your room. Are there any things you would like to change about it? Make those changes now. When it feels right to you, let this expression and place go as the orange misty light begins to obscure your work.

Feel a gentle descent as the light begins to fade from your sphere. The screen of your mind returns to normal coloring and then shrinks back to its normal size.

Count yourself up to waking consciousness.

Give yourself clearance and balance. Ground and center as needed. Write down your experience.

Contemplation

What are the underlying feelings that came out when you expressed yourself in the space? What was the process of expression like for you? Will you try and recreate a part of your room of expression in the physical world? How did you feel after you had expressed what is inside of you?

The Blessing Cord

DREAM

The twenty-ninth bead of the blessing cord is the blessing of dream. It is the blessing of Water in Yesod. Dreams both waking and sleeping can help us in so many ways. Psychological thought says dreams are our subconscious trying to sort out all the things we observed and thought during the day and any underlying conflicts within ourselves. Every dream holds symbolism that helps us work out our unresolved feelings. It is well-documented that people use their dreams to figure out things the waking mind just can't grasp. The subconscious is also the part of us that holds our psychic mind. Dreams can be predictive and perceptive of things we consciously hide from ourselves.

Many inventors and scientists have used their dreams to figure out problems in their work and dream up new solutions. I am sure you have too, whether you know it or not. The issue with a dream is that we can't fully understand its meaning sometimes because we are the dreamer. This is where a good friend comes in handy. It was surprising to me that sometimes in dreams we are like the metaphor "unable to see the forest for the trees." A good friend or loved one can sometimes intuit what your dream symbols mean because they know you well enough.

You may not have a close friend who gets you in this way, and that is okay because there are many other ways to interpret dream symbolism. There are many books on the subject, and I find they have helpful suggestions, but our psyches are not all the same, and this cookie cutter approach doesn't work for everyone. To determine your symbols consciously, you could try listing out everything you remember from your dreams. All the nouns, adjectives, and actions should go into your list. Take this list and begin to free associate. Call out the first word or two that comes to your mind as you hear or see that word. You will get a feel of what the dream symbol means to you by seeing what you associate with it. To help organize your own symbols and what they mean, you can make an alphabetical card file of each dream symbol, or get an address book and write your symbols into the alphabetical sections.

Another way to interpret a dream is to go back into it in meditation. While you are in the dream, everything is alive and responsive. You can have a discussion with your grandmother's table—or anything else—in the dream world and ask it what it means within the dream. In this way we get to interact with our dream symbols and get understanding of the dream at a rapid pace. In this meditation we go back to a dream and speak with its parts to get a greater understanding of the meaning of our symbols. If you don't have a specific dream to analyze, you can ask to be taken to the realm of dreaming so you can experience a new dream and receive a message.

Meditation of Dream

Hold the twenty-ninth bead of the blessing cord, the bead of dream, the blessing of Water in Yesod.

Count yourself down into a meditative state.

The Blessing Cord

Allow the screen of your mind to expand until it is a sphere around you. Feel a sensation of rising as your sphere begins to fill with a misty purple light. Resonate the god name of Yesod: *Sha-dai El-chai.*

As the purple light begins to clear, you find yourself inside the dream you want to interpret, or if it is your intention, a new dream. Everything in this dream can speak and communicate with you. Colors, inanimate objects, animals, people, and whatever symbols you see or experience you can talk to and have them respond.

Begin with the nearest symbol. Say hello to it and ask what it is doing inside your dream. What is its meaning within the dream? Ask if it has a particular message for you in this dream. Take what it tells you at face value and ask it any questions you need clarity about. When you feel like you and the symbol have had a complete conversation, thank it for its help. Then move on to the next symbol and repeat the process. The more you interact with the dream, the more you will understand what the dream as a whole means. Don't limit yourself to just going symbol-by-symbol; you can also ask the whole dream to explain what it means for you.

If any dream symbol seems reluctant or doesn't talk at all, talk to another symbol and ask it to explain the other. Ask another symbol why that one wasn't willing or able to converse with you.

When you feel as though you have gotten the message from this dream, conjure forth the misty purple light to surround you again until the dream is obscured. You feel a slight gentle descent as the light fades from view. The screen of your mind becomes its normal color and shrinks back to its normal size.

Count yourself up into waking consciousness.

Give yourself clearance and balance. Ground and center as needed. Write down your experience.

Contemplation

Consider the symbols your dreams present you: Are there ones that appear in your dream multiple times? What do they signify to you? When you think about your dream, how could it be interpreted in response to what you are experiencing right now in your life? Do you have specific symbols that happen when you are getting a dream that is beyond the normal? What would your symbol be for a dream that was a message from spirit?

BLOOD

The thirtieth bead of the blessing cord is the blessing of blood, the blessing of Water in Malkuth. Blood is the river that passes through the generations. Our blood has passed through our ancestors, through us, and onto the descendants who come after us. It is this river of blood that moves through us and gives us the ancestral patterns and memories of our people. Our blood holds within it the memories of all the ancestors who have gone before and all the memories of our descendants in the future as well.

When we talk about our family, we say "they're my blood" or use the adage "blood is thicker than water." We acknowledge that our blood ties us to our people. Many have postulated that our past life memories could also be memories from our blood ancestors, passed to us like the instincts of birds to return to the same places as their ancestors. Whether this is a genetic transmission of information or a morphogenic field impression or something else doesn't matter. It is true that we have information, patterns, and "blueprints" that are passed to us through the "river" of blood that flows through time.

We are deeply connected to our family and the information passed through the blood, both good and bad. Qualities like a strong determination, optimism, and decisiveness, as well as a weakness for sweets, want for a steady job instead of self-employment, or alcoholism, are all passed through this connection of blood and can be awakened within us. They give us both the peculiar talents that delight us and the addictions that plague us.

The best thing about this river of blood is that you can commune with it in your meditations to be able to go back and see why a pattern is within your psyche and change it, if you so desire. You can also go back and activate talents from your ancestors to deal with your life in the present. You are the product of a thousand loving choices, and these ancestors have a vested interest in both celebrating the gifts and transforming the harmful patterns that may have been passed to you.

In this meditation we visit the river of blood and use it to commune with the ancestors and the patterns of your bloodline. You have the opportunity to call forth the gifts and talents of your ancestors and transform the patterns harmful to you.

Meditation of Blood

Hold the thirtieth bead on the blessing cord, the blessing of blood, the bead of Water in Malkuth.

Count yourself down into a meditative state.

Allow the screen of your mind to expand around you, forming a sphere. Feel the slight shift as a garden begins to grow up around you in the sphere of your mind. Resonate the god name of Malkuth: *Ah-do-nai Ha-ah-retz*

Explore your garden. You find a cave within the garden that leads deeper into the earth of your consciousness. As you walk into the cave, it spirals deeper and deeper. Finally the cave opens up into a cavern with a river flowing through it. This river is a bright red and blue. As you come closer, you can hear a heartbeat. Listen for your own heartbeat and allow it to attune to the rhythm of the river. Step up to the edge and dip your fingers into the flow. Tell it your intention to connect through it to your ancestors. Share if you have a particular intention to awaken or transform talents and patterns that are passed to you from the ancestors.

Feel if the river is ready to connect to you. If it is, step into the flow of the river of blood. As you get to waist depth, turn into the flow moving toward you. Ask to know where the pattern you want to release began. You may have an ancestor rise up from the river or you may see it played out on the surface or in the depths for you to view. See why this pattern started and why it has continued. You can trace this pattern down the flow from your ancestors to see why it continued in your family. Follow what you see until it comes to your generation.

Acknowledge why this pattern continues in your life now. Explain why you want to change this pattern that no longer serves you and your descendants. Thank the pattern for the aid it has given those who went before and then ask that it be transformed and released, putting your intention behind it. What is the effect within the river? Does the pattern boil out? Does it just fade? Thank the river for this healing and awareness.

Ask the river to show you the pattern you want to foster in your life. It may be a talent of an ancestor or their knowledge. Call this up from the blood. An ancestor may rise to talk to you from the blood or the pattern may appear on the surface of the river or in its depths. Ask to see how this pattern originated. See how it has served your ancestors in the past. Thank it for helping your ancestors and ask that it be re-awakened in you. Dip your hands into the waters of the river of blood and scoop up the pattern and pour it over your body to absorb it. Feel the pattern as it mixes and mingles with your own blood and spirit. If an ancestor rose up from the river, you may embrace and merge to gain the pattern and awaken it within you. Thank the pattern for being with you and fill it with light so you can pass it on to your descendants in the river.

When you are finished, leave the river. Give thanks one more time to the river and your ancestors and descendants for their aid and love. Turn back and walk out of the cave into the garden of Malkuth. Return to where you entered, and the garden fades around you. Allow it to fade as you feel a slight shift. The screen of your mind returns to its normal size.

Count yourself up into waking consciousness.

Give yourself clearance and balance. Ground and center as needed. Write down your experience.

Contemplation

What are the gifts you have received through your blood? What are the weaknesses passed to you through your blood? In what ways could these strengths be weaknesses and what ways can these weaknesses be strengths? What will you leave to those who receive the river of blood after you?

STILLNESS

The thirty-first bead on the blessing cord is the blessing of stillness. It is the blessing of Earth in Kether. Stillness is a feeling of centeredness and active peace. From this "place" of stillness, we can see how things in our lives are going to move. We can see the rhythm and cadence of all that is going on in our lives without being unbalanced by it.

I am not sure where I heard it or read it, but when Shiva Lord of the Dance was described, he was said to be the stillness of the center and the whirling cosmic dance. He was both in motion and centered in stillness. This has always stuck with me. I know that ecstatic dance has sometimes put me in this place where I could move my body, yet my spirit was feeling centered stillness. Stillness is that clear, uncomplicated awareness of being. Some people feel this in passive meditation when the mind is clear. The dancing Shiva has it while his body spins and his center is calm like the eye of a storm.

The Wheel of Fortune, one of the major arcana tarot cards, depicts a wheel going round. One of the things I counsel with the Wheel of Fortune is that where you place your focus changes how the wheel affects you: If you are focused on the outside of the wheel, you experience a roller coaster of experience. On the high part of the wheel you are lucky, your life couldn't be better, everything is coming up roses, and you get so excited you just can't stand it. At the bottom of the wheel, you are at your worst: life sucks, you have the whole world on your shoulders, and you are at your most depressed. The wheel can make us feel like we are almost bipolar with highs of mania and lows of depression.

This is what we experience on the outside of the wheel. In the center of the wheel is the axle around which it rotates. It is the stillness in the center of the dance of this cycle. From the center you can feel the up and the down without it moving you out of your center. You can have the luck and adversity and neither shakes you out of your equilibrium. You are part of the dance, but you have the stillness and centering to deal with all the twists and turns of the wheel. All of the cycle pivots around you instead of the other way around. The center of the wheel is the stillness we need to maintain to learn all that the Wheel of Fortune, of life, has to teach us.

When we act from this place of centered stillness, we are like Shiva dancing. We find the rhythm of the dance and are not unbalanced by its motion. From a place of stillness we can observe and predict the next steps. All our parts are aligned in stillness, and we feel greater unity with all of creation.

Meditation of Stillness

Hold the thirty-first bead of the blessing cord, the bead of stillness, the Earth of Kether.

Count yourself down into a meditative state.

Visualize the screen of your mind expanding into a sphere around you. You feel a sense of rising as your sphere begins to fill with radiant prismatic light. Resonate the god name of Kether: *Eh-heh-e-yeh.*

The radiant light flows through you, making your spirit body feel fluid as you become one with the light. This place is timeless and yet contains within it all times. Around you images flash of your past, but you feel a disconnection from these experiences. You are a silent observer on the outside of your time-stream. Focus your mind and intention to see a time where you felt the stillness.

See the time you felt stillness before you. You are an outside observer of yourself. Observe what you are doing. Look at your posture and even observe the energies that emanate from you as you feel stillness. When you feel satisfied that you have observed enough from the outside, merge with this past self. Feel what they feel. See what they see. What are you thinking about? What are you feeling? Where in your body do you feel your stillness the most? How are you dealing with the current situation? Draw your spirit self into the place of stillness within this past self. Observe how it feels to be completely one with this stillness. Feel how everything around it flows and dances while it remains the pivot point of it all. Now that you have found this stillness, know that you can return to it at any time.

Project yourself back out to be an outside observer again. Move back into the white radiant light of the place of timelessness that is all times. Set your intention to see a time in your past, where you had lost this stillness and the dance was swinging you out of control. See this time before you. Again you are an outside observer. Watch your past self lose their stillness. Observe what your past self is doing and going through. Feel and observe the energies that emanate from you. What are your posture and expression like? When you feel ready, project yourself inside your past self. Observe and experience what losing stillness feels like. Why is this happening? You are just an observer, so you can disconnect from these feelings and reconnect to your intuition. What is it saying to your past self? What is the lesson of this time?

Now feel your past self's body. Even in this time of unbalance, can you find the stillness? Where is it now? Connect deeply to the stillness and allow it to spread from this place where you found it. Change the scene of you losing stillness until your past body and your present "body" are in the stillness once more. Feel things calm as you regain your equilibrium. See and observe how the scene changes when you are in alignment with your stillness. Move again outside your past self, leaving behind the sense of stillness. Observe how everything you experienced from the outside has changed. The energies flowing off you and your posture have changed. You have not changed the past, only the way your present self interacts with it.

Step back into the white radiant light that is timelessness and all times. Know that you can find your stillness in any situation by taking a deep breath and focusing your mind to where your stillness lives within your body. The images of your past selves fade, and the light grows more intense. Then it begins to fade and you feel a slight descent as your screen of your mind returns to its natural color. The screen recedes to its normal size.

Count yourself up into waking consciousness.

Give yourself clearance and balance. Ground as needed. Write down your experience.

Contemplation

When do you most feel the stillness? What throws you out of your stillness? How do you regain stillness after you have been thrown out of it?

CONCENTRATION

The thirty-second bead on the blessing cord is the blessing of concentration. It is the Earth of Chokmah. This blessing brings forth the focus we need to be able to be effective magicians and spiritual seekers. Many different spiritual and magickal traditions have the beginning meditation of focusing all of your concentration on one thing and clearing your mind by bringing your focus back to that one thing. Our minds and surroundings are always trying to get our attention, and by focusing our concentration on something, we can clear our minds and increase our ability to do magick.

When I was in the second and third grade and my teacher would be lecturing about something boring, I would focus my attention on one spot and see how long I could hold it. This became a practice when I was bored at home or at school. I would return my focus to the dot in a painting or the tack in my poster and focus all my attention on it. I sometimes couldn't keep the focus for very long and would go into thoughts about cartoons or whatever suited my fancy. My teacher would call it "spacing out." Without knowing it, I was doing beginner methods of concentration meditations.

Different cultures have used focused concentration on one thing to clear the mind in meditation for thousands of years. Some bring focus to our breath, a candle, a mantra, a chakra, and sometimes just the releasing of thoughts. Each time their thoughts wandered, they would bring their concentration back to the focus.

With breath meditation, you focus your thoughts on your breath. This could be on your normal breath or focusing on counted inhalations and exhalations. Normal breath makes you focus on your natural breath. Counted breaths have a certain number for each inhalation, exhalation, and sometimes the pauses in-between: for example, breathing in for four, holding your breath for four, exhaling for four, and then holding out for four counts and repeating the cycle.

Many Craft teachings start you out with concentration on a candle flame. You focus your concentration on the candle and try to think only of the candle. Sometimes you even let your eyes close and see how long you can hold the image of the candle in your mind. This builds both your concentration skills and the ability to visualize.

Mantra is a Hindu and Buddhist practice of focusing our attention on a group of words or one word. Usually a mala or grouping of beads is used to count how many times it is said. The Catholic Rosary could be said to be a mantra practice since it is a group of words said over and over with concentration. There are many types of mantras for multiple purposes. For this concentration practice, you can use one of the seed sound mantas like OM (introduced in the "Word" chapter). You can also use an affirmation which focuses concentration and also affirms the reality that you want to achieve.

One of the practices I loved from *Kundalini Awakening: A Gentle Guide to Chakra Activation and Spiritual Growth* by

John Selby is to focus your attention on a specific chakra in your body. Where our concentration goes, our energy flows. This is a gentle way of awakening chakras by simply focusing our attention on them. The attention sends our energy to that chakra. Usually this is done first by a balancing chakra meditation, then focusing on one chakra, followed by another balancing to smooth out the energy.

When we are concentrating on anything, it is okay for our minds to wander as long as when we become aware that we have wandered, we return back to the focus of our concentration. Having wandering thoughts isn't failure any more than having fatigue from exercise is; it's a natural part of the process of practicing concentration. As you continue working with concentration over time, you will be able to focus for longer and longer periods of time, just like building up a muscle. This is an important spiritual and magickal skill to learn.

Choose a method to focus on for this meditation. Breath, a visualized candle, or mantra work best for this meditation. A great mantra is the god name of this sephira: *Yod-heh-vauv-Heh*. Set a timer for your practice of concentration. You can build up from a short two minutes to fifteen or more.

Meditation of Concentration.

Hold the thirty-second bead on the blessing cord, the bead of concentration, the blessing of Earth in Chokhmah.

Count yourself down into a meditative state.

Allow the screen of your mind to expand around you to form a sphere. Resonate the god name of Chokmah: *Yod heh vauv Heh.*

Focus your concentration on your breath, a visualized candle, or a mantra. Gently allow your concentration to rest upon this focus. Be gentle with yourself if you begin to think or daydream and just bring your concentration back to your focus. Let your focus be your whole world as you gently release all other thoughts. Let them drift away like a released helium balloon, like clouds on the breeze. Keep your concentration on your focus until your timer sounds.

Know that concentration is like a muscle. The more you work with it, the stronger and more enduring it gets. Every time you concentrate your mind, you are getting better at it.

Feel a gentle descent and let your screen of the mind shrink back to normal size.

Count yourself up to waking consciousness.

Give yourself clearance and balance. Ground and center as needed. Write down your experience.

.

Contemplation

What steals your concentration and distracts you from your focus? Is there a thought that comes up a lot to steal away your focus? What do you concentrate on the most in your life? Does that focus of concentration embody where you want to go with your life? What goals do you want to concentrate and focus on?

PATIENCE

The thirty-third bead on the blessing cord is the blessing of patience. It is the blessing of Earth in Binah. There are three elements that must be invested into any manifestation: space, energy, and time. When we work on creating something, we make space for it to exist, we devote our energy and focus to its creation, and we give it time to form. This last one has the blessing of patience ingrained within it. It can also be the most difficult of the three.

We can start to have unrealistic expectations of manifestation. Not every process is as quick as our Amazon order with overnight shipping. This desire for instant gratification of our desires has led us as a people to become more demanding and entitled.

We put this expectation not only onto our manifestation, but also onto ourselves. My partner Steve likes to use the example from the movie *Young Sherlock Holmes,* where Watson comes in to an angry Sherlock cussing out himself for not being able to master the violin. Watson asks "How long have you been playing it?" Sherlock answers something like "Two days! Can you believe I haven't mastered it yet?"

This is a fictional account, of course, but a great example of how unrealistic expectations lead us away from the patient creation of a truly magickal manifestation. Some things take longer to manifest. We have to sometimes devote ourselves and our patience to the goal and keep working on each step along the way. The road can be winding, and we sometimes can lose focus and hope. We will never see the outcome if we don't continue down the path. This takes patience.

I spent years helping kids in group homes, training them to become better people, to adopt strategies that would help them through life. I knew their success could be a reality and would patiently correct behaviors until they reached a modicum of success. I found over the years that it was okay and natural to lose patience every once and a while, to lose our faith in the manifestation, as long as we can return to that patience and hope and begin again. Much like the practices of mindful meditation, sometimes we get distracted or thrown off, and that is okay as long as we return to our focus. That's not a failure to meditate; it's part of the process and the practice of meditation.

In his book *The New Hermetics*, Jason Augustus Newcomb gives a mudra trigger exercise to program during your meditation so you can access more patience and tranquility in any situation. The mudra of tranquility and patience is to connect your thumb and middle finger at the tips while the rest of your fingers are relaxed and open. The middle finger is the finger of Saturn and the element of earth; both are very patient energies. In this meditation we make this mudra even stronger by making it a trigger for patience and tranquility. You can use this mudra to gain patience in any situation and invoke your tranquility.

Meditation of Patience

Hold the thirty-third bead of the blessing cord, the bead of the Earth of Binah, the bead of patience.

Count yourself down into a meditative state.

Allow the screen of your mind to expand to create a sphere around you. Feel a rising sensation as the sphere begins to lose all illumination, until you are surrounded by a black endless void. Resonate the god name of Binah: *Yod Heh Vauv Heh El-oh-heem.*

In this black endless void, conjure up a time where you were not patient. Observe this memory like a watcher from the outside. What was your posture? What were your hopes in that moment? Did you think that they could become true? Had you lost faith in your ability to manifest? Were you bored with what was going on? Were you frustrated? Reacting to a stimulus? Why do you think you lost patience and tranquility in this moment?

Rewind time to the beginning of the scene. Imagine what would have happened if you had been patient. Imagine yourself filled with patience and tranquility, doing what needed to be done in that moment and feeling peace that all will happen as it needs to happen, all your needs met.

When you are finished with this scene, release it. Go to a time where you felt like you had a great amount of patience. Observe how you felt. What was different from the first scene? How was it better and more tranquil?

Really feel the energy of patience and begin to hold your hands in the patience and tranquility mudra. Imagine your patience and tranquility multiplying a thousand times its usual strength.

Charge this mudra with the following statement: "I program this hand position as my patience and tranquility trigger. When I hold my hands like this, I will instantly feel patient and tranquil. I will do my work of the moment with faith that all my needs are met for the highest good, harming none."

Feel the patience and tranquility. Release your mudra. Know that this feeling is always there when you need it. Your screen returns to its normal shape and size.

Count yourself back up to waking consciousness.

Give yourself clearance and balance. Ground and center as needed. Write down your experience.

Contemplation

What throws you out of patience and tranquility? Why do you choose to let it get to you? Are you continuing with all the steps you need to do to get to your goal while being patient?

GRATITUDE

The thirty-fourth bead in the blessing cord is the blessing of gratitude. It is the blessing of Earth in Chesed. As I write this, it is November, and in a couple of weeks we will have our Thanksgiving holiday here in America. I am always reminded at this time of an article I read about a man whose meaning of Thanksgiving changed when he reversed the words into Giving Thanks. He went on about how he changed his life by starting a practice of sending out thank you cards at Thanksgiving to anyone he thought had helped him. This season always reminds me of the power of gratitude. This blessing is one of the keys to a happy life.

Gratitude has been proven by psychologists to make people more alert, enthusiastic, determined, optimistic, happy, and energetic. Gratitude makes us more aware of all the good things in our lives and we begin to see every opportunity as a new blessing. Gratitude has a powerful magnetic quality as well. When we are grateful, we attract more of what we are grateful for. The universe is always listening to what we are thinking and saying. It hears our every thought as a prayer. When we are grateful, we are praying for all the blessings of life. Gratitude charges these thoughts and amplifies our manifestation. Many spiritual and mental manifestation programs say to be thankful for whatever it is that you are trying to manifest even if it is not yet in your life. This act of gratitude supercharges the manifestation to bring happiness and satisfaction.

Gratitude can be difficult in many situations. This is when we must turn our minds to working on contemplating "What good can come out of this situation?" "What can I learn from this?" or "How can I/we/the world benefit from this?" Even after we have contemplated, we may not see a way to be grateful for the situation. These times of trouble outline the better times with such stark contrast. They at least help us recognize when times are good and to be grateful for them.

Some of the ways you can improve your awareness and gratitude is to practice it. Start your journal every day with a number of things you are grateful for. Put up a sign or reminder to check-in with what your grateful for. Decide on a trigger in your environment that whenever you see it, you will think of something you are grateful for. Wear a piece of jewelry that reminds you to be practice gratitude. Notice when people say "thank you" and tell them what you are thankful for about them or the situation you are in. Set a period of days to write a thank-you card to someone every day.

The practice seems so easy, and that is why it is hard. Sometimes it takes thinking of a perspective unlike our own to see all that we have to be thankful for. Putting on the head of someone who has very little in the way of resources can help you be grateful for all that you do have and maybe even share a bit with that person or the world.

The most powerful of all the gratitude practices is just giving to those who are in need. This doesn't have to be a grand gesture; it could be just doing the dishes for a busy spouse. Or giving thanks to things that have served you well in the past, but are no longer necessary to your life and then giving them to someone who can use them more. You get to say "thank you" to the world with this gesture and see someone else gain happiness from your act.

Meditation of Gratitude

Hold the thirty-forth bead of your blessing cord, the bead of gratitude, the bead of the blessing of Earth in Chesed.

Count yourself down into a meditative state.

Allow the screen of your mind to expand to create a sphere around you. Feel a rising sensation as sky-blue or electric-blue light begins to fill the sphere. Resonate the god name of Chesed: *El.*

Call out in your mind to your higher self to come and be with you in this meditation. Look above you to the great expanse of the universe and see a spot of bluish-white light descending and growing larger. This light is like a small star that comes closer to the top of your head and stops about six feet above you. This star is a representation of your higher self. Thank your higher self for being present and send up to it a breath of gratitude for being with you and a part of you. Feel the bliss of your connection.

Bring your attention to the screen of your mind before you. Call up on the screen of your mind someone you feel grateful for. See them before you. Call out to their higher self to be present with you. Ask if this person is open to a gift of gratitude. If not, just thank them with your words, knowing that you are subjectively communicating your thanks to that person.

If they are willing to accept a gift of gratitude, tell them thanks for what they have done for you. Then imagine you are gathering the blue light from around you into a ball of light between your hands. Say to yourself: "I create this gift and blessing of gratitude to be what your higher self thinks you need for the highest good, harming none."

Raise the ball up above your head and breathe up to your higher self asking for its blessing on this gift. You may feel a tingle as the ball is blessed. It may change color or become a symbolic object of what it is this person needs. Be aware of how it changes, especially if it changes into something, as this may guide you in expressing your gratitude to this person in the physical world.

Give the gift to the person and say "thank you" again. End the exchange with a "blessed be." Wave farewell to the person and their higher self. They fade from the screen of your mind.

Give thanks by breathing up to your higher self for its help in this gift and blessing.

Become aware of all the blue light rising around you to obscure this place. The blue light begins to fade as you feel a slight descent. The screen of your mind begins to go back to its normal size and color.

Count yourself up into waking consciousness.

Give yourself clearance and balance. Ground and center as needed. Write down your experience.

Contemplation

How can I incorporate gratitude into my life? In this moment, what am I grateful for? What good can come out of this situation? What can I learn from this situation? How can I/we/the world benefit from this situation? Who in my life can I show thanks to? How can I give my gratitude back to the world for my blessings?

INDUSTRY

The thirty-fifth bead in the blessing cord is the blessing of industry. It is the blessing of Earth in Malkuth. In this blessing, we take the power of Geburah and apply it to the earthly plane. Industry is the passion for work and creation. Industry is what we do to get all the things we need done done.

When I think of industry, I start to think about some of the people I know who do craft fairs. They personally produce a great deal of product with their many talents. They pack in as much crafting time before the fair as they can. There is a sort of furious fire of creation fueled by this deadline. Industry like this can bring stress because of the intensity of its energy, but it is this power that can help us achieve so much.

One of the things that can hold us back from the blessing of industry is the slowing effect of procrastination. We all avoid that which we feel is annoying or unpleasant, putting it off to the last minute, even though we know it is necessary or good for us. This makes changes more and more difficult. At times when I find myself doing this, I make a list of all the things I know I should do and then rearrange the list for what I don't want to do the most to be at the top. Then I take a day and just do everything I can on the list. I am always amazed how much less time it takes me to get things done than I thought once I just get started.

Another way I stoke the fires of my industry is using the Pomodoro® Technique developed by Francesco Cirillo in the 1980s. Basically you make a list of all the things you need to do. Then you choose one to work on for traditionally 25 minutes, a session called a pomodoro because the timer Francesco used was tomato-shaped, and pomodoro is "tomato" in Italian. During this pomodoro, you focus only on the task at hand. Any time you think of something or want to do something else you write it down on your list and get back to the task you were focusing your pomodoro on. When the timer goes off, you take a three to five minute break and then start a new pomodoro on either the same subject or a new one from your list. After you have done four pomodoro sessions with breaks, you take a longer break that is 15 to 30 minutes. If you finish before the pomodoro is up, it is suggested that you focus on over learning, which is to study something to refresh you memory about it. I just clean if I have extra time in the pomodoro; there is always more cleaning to do.

In this meditation, we take some of the energy and power of Geburah and send it to future moments and times where we need to have the fire of industry. You might want to make a list of the things you need to get a move on about and prioritize them so you are ready with a few instances where you are going to need the blessings of industry. Don't choose more than three things for this meditation because with the get-it-done energy of Geburah, we can also invoke the stress and anger of Geburah and unbalance ourselves. Stress and anger directed toward a positive end can be useful, but too much can be unbalancing. Industry can also be turned into overwork if we aren't careful. Use moderation and your good sense.

Meditation of Industry

Hold the thirty-fifth bead, the bead of the blessing of industry, the blessing of Earth in Geburah. Count yourself down into a meditative state.

Allow the screen of your mind to expand to create a sphere around you. Feel a rising sensation as the sphere fills with a red light. Vibrate the god name of Geburah: *El-oh-heem Gi-boor.*

The red light around you begins to fade and becomes a red sphere of light above you. At any time you can access the energy of Geburah by calling it down from this sphere. Before you, conjure a picture of yourself doing the work that is on your list. See it in as much detail as you can. Ask the image of you doing this work what the reason is that you haven't finished this project. Clear your mind and be open to any answers. It may be that the image changes or begins to talk to you to tell you why. You may get a feeling of knowing. Whatever the reason, forgive yourself for it. You may have a person show up as the reason you have issues getting this done. Forgive this person and embrace them.

Bring your attention back to the image of you doing the work you have put off. Draw down the red energy of Geburah with a breath in, and with your exhale, send it into the image of your work. See your image self surrounded in the red light. As you do, they begin to work harder on getting this project done. Time seems to speed up in the image until you are at the finish of the project. Breathe in more light and send it to the image of the completed project. Begin to feel what it is like to have the project done. Use all your senses. Know that this project will be completed in the proper time. Release the image knowing that as it fades, it goes into manifestation.

You may repeat this process with two other projects or continue to your return. When you feel you are done, the red light again fills your view, obscuring all else. You feel a gentle descent as the red light fades. Your sphere returns to the shape and size of the screen of the mind.

Count yourself up into waking consciousness.

Give yourself clearance and balance. Ground and center yourself as needed. Write down your experience.

Contemplation

What are you procrastinating on? How do you feel about what you are procrastinating on? What are your reasons why you don't want to do it? What actions will move you forward on your path? Can you change the way you think about your task so that you enjoy it or at least are relieved when it is done?

GENEROSITY

The thirty-sixth bead of the blessing cord is the blessing of generosity. This is the Earth of Tiphereth. Tiphereth has an energy that brings forth our True Will or our Great Work, what we came here to this world to complete, and how we choose to answer that calling. You can see the hallmarks of True Will by looking for how it serves not only the person, but also the web of life. It takes a generosity of spirit to be able to do this Great Work as a gift to the divine that is within us all. This generosity shows our nobility of spirit and our inner sovereignty.

Generosity comes from the Latin word *generōsus*, meaning "of noble birth." A good noble took care of their community by allocating resources, planning, implementing, and educating. They did so because without the community, they would not be in the exalted position they were in. To take that into our spiritual realms, a good noble or sovereign is sufficiently in control of their own lives that they can give of their time, energy, resources, and wisdom to help those are less fortunate or in their charge. We each have this sovereignty within us, no matter our wealth, class, time, schedule, or energy level. We can adopt the noble path of generosity and give in the name of the gods. They love when we make these types of offerings and help to refill us so we can give again.

The community you aid with your generosity or your Great Work may take many forms, and not all of them are on a grand global scale. It could be once a year giving a homeless person an old jacket or a tent. It could be helping with the school bake sale for your kids' marching band. You may feel called to go to an impoverished community or disaster area and offer your help and expertise. Generosity doesn't have to be a grand gesture. You can generously give a smile or a compliment. You can buy a friend a coffee or tea because they are having a tough time. Give a friend a book you enjoyed that you think they will also.

The blessing of generosity teaches us how to give and share our gifts with community. Many cultures and religions have tithes that they give to their religious institutions or charities. A tithe is a percentage of your income that you give back to the community with no expectation of return. Even if they didn't expect return, they still might get it in the form of the rituals of the temple or from the gods themselves. You may also want to give a tithe of time in service to your community, if you do not have physical wealth to offer.

Generosity can feel like a sacrifice of time, energy, or resources that could be used for yourself and your goals. We turn to the solar gods of Tiphereth for our model. Most of the solar gods participate in a cycle where they sacrifice themselves to the land or its people. Many of the pagan solar gods sacrifice themselves so that we may take in their blessings by consuming a part of them. The young Oak King is sacrificed by the older Holly King at the summer solstice to bring his energy into the land so the fields will ripen. This also brings about the turning of the "wheel of the year" as the darker time of less daylight begins. The change of

The Blessing Cord

wheat from green to gold symbolizes the God's energy in the land. From his sacrifice, the wheat and all the plants ripen. This is an archetypal example of the generosity of the gods. We pagans are not alone in this; the Christian faith's Christ sacrificed himself to take on the world's sin. The rite of transubstantiation is to make the wine and host into the blood and body of Christ. People take some of the energy of his holiness, his sacrifice, into themselves with the sacrament. We pagans have the Great Rite in token, where we drink in the blessings of the gods after an athame is used to gather energy and is brought into the wine as a symbolic ritual of the male giving up his seed and energy to the womb of life.

These divinities show their generosity by giving freely of what they have to help their people, just as the Sun, the symbol of Tiphereth, gives freely of its light and warm. We are only seeds of gods and don't have the same expectations because we are human. Our sacrifice to generosity doesn't have to be big; it doesn't necessarily mean giving up something that we need or use.

Generosity has great benefits as well. It has been scientifically proven to make people happier. I have never met an unhappy generous person. It improves your self-esteem and feelings of self-worth. It can connect you deeply to what your Great Work is in this world, something beyond just your vocation or career.

In this meditation, we move into the energies of Tiphereth and ask: "How can I offer up a service in generosity?" Our answer comes from our own Holy Guardian Angel, the Watcher Self, the god seed within us.

Your answer may come in the meditation or be an encounter with a need you can fulfill in the days after the meditation. Take this chance to be an answered prayer for someone else.

Meditation of Generosity

Hold the thirty-sixth bead, the bead of the blessing of generosity, the blessing of Earth in Tiphereth.

Count yourself down into a meditative state.

Allow the screen of your mind to expand into a sphere around you. Feel a rising sensation as your sphere begins to fill with radiant golden-yellow light. Vibrate the god name of Tiphereth: *Yod-heh-vauv-heh el-oh-ah Vah-dah-ath.*

As the golden light surrounds you, call out to your Holy Guardian Angel. You may see it as a golden ball above you or coming toward you. They may take on any appearance that they wish. Thank your Holy Guardian Angel for being with you in this time.

Ask them, "How can I offer up a service in generosity?"

They may give you a feeling, a word or phrase, some sage advice, or an image of someone. They may also say nothing at all.

Ask what you can give to your Holy Guardian Angel in thanks for its help and communion. You may be surprised at the answer. It may ask you to do a generous service for yourself or someone else.

Ask any other questions you might have about becoming a more generous person. Know that your Holy Guardian Angel has heard you and is willing to guide you

The Blessing Cord

after this meditation to a situation where your generosity is needed.

Thank your Holy Guardian Angel again. The golden light begins to fill the screen of the mind around you, obscuring your Holy Guardian Angel from view. The golden light begins to fade, and the screen of your mind returns to its normal size.

Count yourself up to waking consciousness.

Give yourself clearance and balance. Ground and center yourself as needed. Write down your experience.

Contemplation

What can you give back to your community? What types of need call out to you? Do you look at what you want to do and what the need is in the world and make a compromise of the two? How can you be a more generous person?

CONNECTION

The thirty-seventh bead on the blessing cord is the blessing of connection. This is the blessing of Earth in Netzach. We live in an interconnected world. There is not an action that can be taken that doesn't have an effect on the world around us. We are a collection of molecules swimming in a sea of other molecules. We label things with words and illusionary boundaries so that we can consciously function. We are all part of the oneness of all creation, yet we dim down our perspective so we can make choices for the part of creation we "control." Without these words of binding, we can't express what it is we are consciously speaking about.

This is why when we have our own vision of oneness where we experience a dissolving of all barriers we can't seem to put it into words that others would understand. People who have had this experience of being part of the Mystery of the All, more than just a discrete separate piece, have a hard time explaining it to those who haven't felt it fully. This is perhaps why some traditions call it a Mystery.

Breaking the One down into parts is how our conscious mind makes sense of the swirling chaos of oneness. We separate things in our mind by naming them, placing limits on what they are and are not, and putting the rest of what they are out of our minds. We do this so we can focus on a particular part of the All at a time. Without this, we could not do our work in the world because we would be constantly distracted by all the information coming in from all directions.

It is amazing how the universal consciousness lets us have our personal will about our connection. We can slip into a closed circuit of our personal consciousness and not have to be aware of the world around us. I would say that we can recede inside our own heads, but even this is an illusion, for our minds and spirits are all parts of the One. We shutter ourselves into thinking that we can only be aware of ourselves and whatever we can see from our own perspective.

We can dissolve these barriers at a whim. Often the work of the magician is to be able to melt the self-imposed barriers so we can gather energy and influence. We do this through connection and merging. An exercise that comes to mind from Raymond Buckland's *Scottish Witchcraft* is to get an ordinary stone and open up to connection to it. Imagine the barriers between you and it becoming more and more hazy. Feel the energy and spirit of the stone and begin to have an exchange of energy. You could use this to pack a stone with energy, or you could do it to recharge yourself. This small exercise leads to opening up to energies of the earth or a tree and having an exchange of power.

This merging and connection also leads me to speak about a trick of invisibility I learned. Imagine yourself and your consciousness, the lines of the boarders of your body coming into your mind. Begin to imagine them blurring and becoming one with the scenery all around you until you are as one with all that is around you. Because you have let go of your conscious limits and boundaries, you begin to become unnoticeable to those who use their conscious mind to see the world. You disappear, just a part of the greater All.

In this meditation, we return to the garden landscape of Netzach and try merging to connect to all that is around us in the garden. Then we return to our "separated" state to get a sense of the power of the blessing of connection.

Meditation of Connection

Hold the thirty-seventh bead of your blessing cord, the bead of connection, the bead of Earth in Netzach.

Count yourself down into a meditative state.

Allow the screen of your mind to expand until it is a sphere around you. Feel the sensation of rising as a green light begins to fill the sphere around you. Resonate the god name of Netzach: *Yod-heh-vau-Heh Tza-ba-oth.*

The green light surrounds you and becomes a mist. As the green mist begins to fade, you see a garden. This is the Garden of the Gods, a sacred space where you can connect to all of nature. Greenery abounds around you. Take some time to observe the plants and animals. Take in all the sensory details of the garden. What does it smell like? What does the grass feel like beneath your feet? What sounds do you hear?

Find a comfortable place in the garden. It could be leaning your back against a tree or a warm spot in the grass. When you have your spirt body comfortable in that spot, begin to imagine the boundaries of your spirit body blending and blurring. You are becoming one with the scenery around you. Your skin blends like in a painting, and you begin to sense yourself becoming one and merging with all the energies around you. You may experience the energies of connection to nature even more fully in this blended state. Feel the sea of energy that makes up the garden. Feel the vibration of the energy all around you. Trade energy with whatever is around you. Feel any tense or unhealthy energies for you taken on by that which can use or recycle that energy. As this energy moves out, newer and fresher energy that the world around you has to spare flows naturally flows in.

When you are done, visualize the boundaries of your spirit body firming, disconnecting from the blended state. Your skin becomes solid once more. As you become more separate from the energies you merged with, know that at any time you can return to this connected feeling. You are always a part of this amazing creation.

Green misty light fills the area, obscuring it from view. The green begins to fade as you feel a gentle descent. The screen of your mind returns to its normal size.

Count yourself up into waking consciousness.

Give yourself clearance and balance. Ground and center as needed. Write down your experience.

Contemplation

How can you better connect with nature? What energies do you need to connect with in order to join the pattern of what you want to create in your life and the world? Why do we separate from the All? Is there another purpose to this disconnect that has nothing to do with conscious organizing?

The Blessing Cord

PLANNING

The thirty-eighth bead on the blessing cord is the blessing of planning. It is the blessing of Earth in Hod. Hod has to do with our mental capabilities and mental faculties. When we apply this energy to the power of earth, we get planning. The blessing of planning helps organize our steps so we are more likely to get to our goals. This being said, don't be afraid to change plans when you meet up with synchronicity or guidance that the goal isn't for you. They say a plan is only as good as the first battle, and then it must change and adapt.

One of the concepts brought up in most human religions is that of the Divine Plan: that we are all here for a reason, we have a purpose, and the more we accept that we are working on this purpose, the more we are doing our Great Work. I feel like most of the people I read for are asking "what is my purpose?" or "why am I here?" These readings always make me laugh because they almost always say "well, I knew that" or "that is good confirmation" when the answers come through. Our plan or purpose from the divine is not just one thing or the lesson from one instance. Our purpose is what we naturally choose, mixed with our aspirations to make ourselves better people.

The "master plan" or "divine plan" is made up of all the choices and goals we make on a day-to-day basis, not just what we consciously choose, but what we choose with our whole being. We are constantly being guided by our Holy

Guardian Angel and our psychic self. All the goals we work toward teach us more about ourselves and what our Great Work really is. The events that happen, the signs, our personal development, and how the goal changes over time can teach us a great deal about the lessons of our "Divine Plan."

The first step to having a plan is knowing what it is you want to accomplish. What are your goals? There are two types of goals: means goals and end goals. A means goal is a specific goal as a step towards getting you to a larger goal, like getting a job to pay the bills so you can support yourself while you write the Great American Novel. The hard part of these goals is that you can eventually start to think of them as your end goal, which is a more of the essence of what you want to do with your life: being happy, enjoying your life, feeling accomplished, and doing what makes you feel whole. The end goal is really the essence of what you desire.

To get a better feeling of what the essence of your goals in this lifetime are, here is an exercise I learned from Vishen Lakhiani, CEO of Mind Valley, to get in touch with them. Get out a timer, a piece of paper, and a pen. Separate the paper into three sections using a line of your pen. Write one of these three questions across the top of each section: What do I want to experience in life? Where do I want to grow? What do I want to contribute to the world? When you have done that, set your timer to two minutes and begin to write your answers to the first question. Repeat the process with each question. The timer makes you go with your first instinct by not allowing you to dwell too long on each answer.

Now look over your answers. You may now have a better idea of what it is you want to create in your life. Now that you have seen these answers, you may want to form them into a kind of mission statement. Your mission statement may change over time, but writing it out can clarify your choices that form your plan. If that seems too big for you, formulate what your goal is for the next five years or even just the next year. I like to make a list of my goals for the next year in the time between Samhain (Halloween) and New Year's Day. Up here in the Northern Hemisphere, it is a dark time full of reflection and celebrations with family. It is a good time to start thinking about the goals for the next year and to look back at the last year's goals and how you did on accomplishing them. This can also inform your planning. What type of plan works best for you?

I then like to break up this year-long goal in my planner into goals for the month. This takes work to separate out what are reasonable steps I can accomplish to get to my goal every month. (I say "reasonable" steps because sometimes when we are in the planning phase, we can get a little overzealous and overwork ourselves.) Always incorporate breaks from your work into your plan. The length of the breaks is proportionate to what it is you have observed you need to keep your balance. This could be a day off or a week off where you do something fun and relaxing. Breaks are important so we don't have a breakdown. Make sure all these goals are flexible enough that you can change them when needed, not set in stone. Remember that a plan changes once it hits the battlefield. It is okay to change the plan and okay to change our goals when we find they were not exactly what we thought they would be.

There are times where planning seems to fail us and we don't know what the next step is to our goal or even the steps to clear our path to it. We may be stumped on what the goals are and how to get there. The following meditation is a spiritual way to get a vision of a goal and the next step.

Meditation of Planning

Hold the thirty-eighth bead of the blessing cord. The bead of planning, the blessing of Earth in Hod.

Count yourself down into a meditative state.

Allow the screen of your mind to expand until it is a sphere around you. Feel a sensation of rising as your sphere begins to fill with an orange light. Resonate the god name of Hod: *El-oh-heem Tza-ba-oth.*

The orange light surrounds you like a mercurial mist. Ask your guides and guardians to be with you to answer your questions. Ask the space around you: "What is the best goal for me right now?"

Clear your mind and stare into the orange mist. A scene or symbol begins to emerge from the mist. You may have a thought, memory, feeling, or hear words in your head describing what your next goal will be like. Note all the sensory details about this answer. Suspend all doubt and take what comes first to your inner vision. Know that if you receive nothing, you may receive it in a dream or synchronicity in the physical world. Have faith in yourself and your process that you will recognize it at the proper time.

Again the orange mist rises and obscures the image or symbol. Your mind clears. Ask your next question of the space around you: "What is the next step that is best for me?"

Again allow the mists to part and show you a vision of what your next step should be. Take in all the sensory details about this answer. Be open to it being something you might have not expected. A sign may show up in your daily life, so be open to perceiving it.

Thank your guides and the energy of this sphere for the answers you have received. State to yourself that you will remember clearly all salient details of this meditation. The orange light rises again to obscure all from view.

Feel a gentle descent as the orange light begins to fade from your sphere. The screen of your mind returns to normal coloring and then shrinks back to its normal size.

Count yourself up to waking consciousness.

Give yourself clearance and balance. Ground and center as needed. Write down your experience.

Contemplation

What do you want to experience in your life? Where do you want to grow? What do you want to contribute to the world? What is the next step towards those things? How can I better plan ahead to reach my goals? What have I learned about what types of planning works best for me? Am I willing to change my plans if necessary?

FORMATION

The thirty-ninth bead on the blessing cord is the blessing of formation. It is the blessing of Earth in Yesod. Yesod is the sephira sometimes called the storehouse of images. This is where all the images, archetypes, patterns, memories—the foundations of our manifestation—are held. It is sometimes attributed to the astral plane, the layer of reality where our own physical world's patterns of manifestation are held. It is the place often called the Foundation of our own world in Malkuth. The images, ideas, and patterns all have the possibility to be manifested within the realm of Malkuth. The patterns of Yesod are our blueprints of what we bring into formation in our lives.

This concept of a plane of energy patterns reminds me of a New Age concept called the causal plane. The term was used by Neo-theosophists, who believed there are four planes of existence: causal, mental, astral, and physical. To make formation in the physical world, we must move our idea or image from the causal plane through the mental and astral and then it has formation within physical reality. As multidimensional beings we can move between these planes in astral travel and in some meditations.

You can think about these planes like the work of a factory. Inspiration occurs in the causal plane. The mental plane is where we draw up the blueprints for whatever we are making. The astral is where resources and energy are brought together in that pattern. Then the physical is our end product. When we "beta test" our physical product and it does not work as we thought or is not quite right, we go "back to the drawing board" to change our blueprint and create a better product.

The energetic planes can be used this way to take something that has manifested in your life and dissolve it by symbolically going back through the factory, taking the whole thing apart and putting it back together in a way that works for your purposes. In this meditation, we will go through the different planes, taking a problem with us. As we bring something back to the causal plane, it dissolves back into its component parts, allowing us to reassemble it according to a new blueprint of our creation.

Meditation of Formation

Hold the thirty-ninth bead of the blessing cord, the bead of formation, the blessing of Earth in Yesod.

Count yourself down into a meditative state.

Allow the screen of your mind to expand until it is a sphere around you. Feel a sensation of rising as your sphere begins to fill with a misty purple light. Resonate the god name of Yesod: *Sha-dai El-chai.*

The purple light grows to a darker shade of purple, like the color of an eggplant. The darker it gets, the closer you are to the plane of the physical. Bring up on the screen of your mind the issue or problem you have been experiencing. Visualize it fully with all of your senses. Say to yourself, "I am now changing this problem." Imagine the problem being encased in a bubble of energy, then shrinking down until you can hold the bubble in your hand.

The Blessing Cord

You can see the representation of your issue inside the bubble.

Intend to take this issue into the causal plane to dissolve this blueprint and create its solution. The purple light around you begins to lighten to a medium range purple like a violet. Feel how your problem has moved with you higher into the astral. Look at it and observe what images and feelings make up its form in the astral level. It may appear more symbolic here.

Intend to move higher and observe how the light around you becomes a light purple. Look again at your problem and see the thoughts that made it up. You may hear them as words or experience them as knowings or images.

Move even higher into the causal plane. The light around you becomes a prismatic white that holds all colors within it. Your problem begins to dissolve in the pure energy of this place. You may feel like you are merging with the plane around you. There is a great peace here and all solutions are possible. Begin to take in this higher vibrational energy and form an image of your problem as solved. Visualize the solution or the end result you truly desire, then begin to descend with your solution.

The light becomes pale purple. Here in the mental plane, form your thoughts about this solution. You may want to say an affirmation of this new end result.

Descend again into the violet light and reinforce images of your end result. Watch as it pulls in energy from the astral plane all on its own, moving towards formation.

Descend again to the astral plane where you are close to the plane of manifestation. See the deep purple light all around you. Let your end result expand until it fills the screen of your mind. Step into the vision and experience it with all your senses. Doing this makes it real for you. Return back into your sphere of the mind with the purple light of Yesod all around you. Allow your end vision to fade and know that it goes to be manifested in the physical world.

Everything around you is obscured by the purple light. You feel a slight gentle descent as the light fades from view. The screen of your mind becomes its normal color and shrinks back to its normal size.

Count yourself up into waking consciousness.

Give yourself clearance and balance. Ground and center as needed. Write down your experience.

Contemplation

What ideas shape what you have created in your life? What long-held beliefs have gotten you to where you are? Do they still serve you? What is it you want to bring into formation?

BODY

The fortieth bead on the blessing cord is the blessing of body. This is the blessing of Earth in Malkuth. Our bodies— no matter their condition—are a true blessing. Many religions discount the body and the physical, seeing them as impure expressions of our nature. They either seek to deny the body or to detach from it. They seek to be of pure spirit or to cast aside the illusion of the body in pursuit of a "higher" experience.

It is my belief that we are incarnated in bodies for a reason. There are lessons to be learned on this plane and our way to learn them is through the body. It is both a vehicle of our journey through Malkuth and also a great teacher of our lessons. The body is our vehicle and medium to experience the pleasure and pain of the physical world. It is the vehicle born of desire and destroyed by it. It is more than just a vehicle of our worldly experience; it is also our teacher in this lifetime.

Our bodies are sending us information all the time. Pleasure and pain tell us more about how to survive in this world. Our heart races when we meet a special someone or beats uncontrollably as we escape from an attacker. Our body relaxes when we meditate, giving us a better ability to tap into the flow of spirit. It tells us when we need healing, rest, nurturing, love, or even when to fight back. Each message the body sends us has layers of meaning. A pain in the neck tells us we are working on something that annoys us and we need to take a break. A pain in our back tells us we should ask for help and not try to solve it all by ourselves, carrying the weight of the world. Hearing loss asks us to examine what it is we don't want to hear and to be more open. There are hundreds of different messages that our body gives us that can help in our healing process and our Great Work. We have only to listen deeply to get more of the message.

This conversation is not just one-sided though. We can ask our body questions to gain more insight in even our day-to-day problems. Think about an issue you have been struggling with. Tune into your body and feel how these thoughts affect your body. Do you feel warm or cold when you hold this thought? Does your heart beat faster or slower? How is your breathing? Where do you feel tension within your body? Asking yourself what you feel in your body can give you information when you know how your body talks to you. Warm and cold can tell us if something is agreeable or not, expansive or contractive, inviting or scary. Your heart and your breath can gauge how excited you are or how peaceful something makes you. Where you feel tension can tell you where this issue sits within you and give you symbolic information about it. For me, a pain in the neck is an annoying trial, a sore foot is not wanting to take the next step, and tired eyes can tell me there is something I don't want to see. These are just a few examples.

The body is part of our evolution in this lifetime, and by beginning our discussion with it, we can learn our world's lessons faster. It is important that we take care of our vehicle and teacher. With exercise and diet, we can make

The Blessing Cord

our bodies stronger to help us channel our spiritual work. Caring for our bodies helps us stay in them longer, learn more lessons, and channel more of the energies of the spirit. Eastern spiritual traditions combine physical exercise with spiritual work. Yoga, qi-gong, and tai chi all are used to balance our body with our spiritual work. Yoga "yokes" the body with the work of the spirit. In our Western traditions, we seem to ignore the body; we need to bring it back so we can find balance. It is the combination that makes us stronger.

In the following meditation we use our awareness to connect deeper to the body. In this deeper connection, we tune into the body's wisdom to receive its messages and to ask about situations and get the answers of sensations.

Meditation of Body

Hold the fortieth bead on the blessing cord, the blessing of body, the bead of Earth in Malkuth.

Count yourself down into a meditative state.

Allow the screen of your mind to expand out around you, forming a sphere. Feel the slight shift as a garden begins to grow up around you in the sphere of your mind. Resonate the god name of Malkuth: *Ah-do-nai Ha-ah-retz.*

Bring your focus away from the earth and turn it inward to your body. Inhale slowly. Focus on the breath as it moves into your nose, down your throat, and into your lungs. When your lungs are full, hold your breath in this fullness. Release it slowly, aware of how it feels to release the air. Exhale until you are empty of breath. Hold your breath out and feel the emptiness in your lungs. Repeat this process, being aware of your breath for a couple more cycles.

Let your awareness gently expand to feel your heart. Be aware of your breath and the beat of your heart. Feel your heartbeat. This is the rhythm of your body. Let your awareness expand as you follow the blood within your body. Let your awareness expand to become aware of your whole body. Your breath, the beat of your heart, and the feeling of your body fill your awareness. Ask in your mind if your body has any messages for you. You may feel your awareness focused on one area of your body. It may be tension, a pain or a tingle that brings your attention. Note the area you are drawn to. Ask what this area of the body means. What is the message of your body in this place? The information may come to you as a feeling, knowing, images, or sounds. Be open to its expression.

If you have a situation you want to get clarity on, ask your body now. Follow your awareness to the place within your body where you feel tension, pain, or tinging. Focus on this place and ask what messages it holds for you. What is your body trying to tell you? Be open to perceptions and let understanding come.

Let your attention come back out of your body to the garden of Malkuth around you. The garden begins to fade as the screen of your mind returns to its natural color and you feel a gentle descent. Your screen shrinks back to its normal size.

Count yourself up into waking consciousness.

Give yourself clearance and balance. Ground and center as needed, Write down your experience.

The Blessing Cord

Contemplation

What do you like about your body? What do you not like? How can you strengthen your body? What lessons have you learned from your body? What do the limitations of your body teach you?

ABOUT THE AUTHOR

Adam Sartwell has practiced witchcraft for over twenty years and is an accomplished psychic reader, healer, and Reiki Master. He and his partners co-founded the Temple of Witchcraft, a religious non-profit where he is Virgo lead minister in charge of the healing ministries, and he helped to found Copper Cauldron Publishing. Find out more at *templeofwitchcraft.org* and *coppercauldronpublishing.com*.